GREAT WESTERN

COUNTY CLASSES

THE CHURCHWARD 4-4-0s, 4-4-2 TANKS AND HAWKSWORTH 4-6-0s

GREAT WESTERN

COUNTY CLASSES

THE CHURCHWARD 4-4-0s, 4-4-2 TANKS AND HAWKSWORTH 4-6-0s

DAVID MAIDMENT

PEN & SWORD
TRANSPORT

AN IMPRINT OF PEN & SWORD BOOKS LTD.
YORKSHIRE – PHILADELPHIA

First published in Great Britain in 2018 by
Pen & Sword Transport
An imprint of Pen & Sword Books Ltd
Yorkshire - Philadelphia

Typeset in Palatino by Aura Technology and Software Services, India
Printed and bound in India by Replika Press Pvt. Ltd.

Pen & Sword Books Ltd incorporates the Imprints of Aviation, Atlas, Family History, Fiction, Maritime, Military, Discovery, Politics, History, Archaeology, Select, Wharncliffe Local History, Wharncliffe True Crime, Military Classics, Wharncliffe Transport, Leo Cooper, The Praetorian Press, Remember When, Seaforth Publishing and Frontline Publishing.

For a complete list of Pen & Sword titles please contact

PEN & SWORD BOOKS LTD
47 Church Street, Barnsley, South Yorkshire, S70 2AS, England
E-mail: enquiries@pen-and-sword.co.uk
Website: www.pen-and-sword.co.uk

Or

PEN AND SWORD BOOKS
1950 Lawrence Rd, Havertown, PA 19083, USA
E-mail: Uspen-and-sword@casematepublishers.com
Website: www.penandswordbooks.com

All David Maidment's royalties from this book will be donated to the Railway Children charity [reg. no. 1058991] [www.railwaychildren.org.uk]

Other books by David Maidment:

Novels (Religious historical fiction)
The Child Madonna, Melrose Books, 2009
The Missing Madonna, PublishNation, 2012
The Madonna and her Sons, PublishNation, 2015

Novels (Railway fiction)
Lives on the Line, Max Books, 2013

Non-fiction (Railways)
The Toss of a Coin, PublishNation, 2014
A Privileged Journey, Pen and Sword, 2015
An Indian Summer of Steam, Pen and Sword, 2015
Great Western Eight-Coupled Heavy Freight Locomotives, Pen and Sword, 2015
Great Western Moguls and Prairies, Pen and Sword, 2016
Southern Urie and Maunsell 2-cylinder 4-6-0s, Pen and Sword, 2016
Great Western Small-Wheeled Double-Framed 4-4-0s, Pen & Sword, 2017
The Development of the German Pacific Locomotive, Pen & Sword 2017
Great Western Large-Wheeled Double-Framed 4-4-0s, Pen & Sword 2017

Non-fiction (Street Children)
The Other Railway Children, PublishNation, 2012
Nobody ever listened to me, PublishNation, 2012

Cover photo:
Hawksworth 'County' 4-6-0, 1000 *County of Middlesex* of Bristol Bath Road, as built at the end of 1945 with large unique double chimney, seen here at Old Oak Common, 5.5.1956 (R.C. Riley)

Back cover:
Churchward 'County' 4-4-0 3836 *County of Warwick* on shed in the 1920s. It was built in 1904 as 3479, and renumbered 3836 in the GW 1912 general locomotive renumbering. (G W Trust)

CONTENTS

PREFACE

Having written books on the Great Western double-framed 4-4-0s in previous Pen & Sword Locomotive Portfolio volumes, I was persuaded to tackle the subject of their contemporary outside cylindered inside framed 4-4-0s and their tank engine derivatives, the 'Counties' and the so-called 'County' 4-4-2 tank engines with similar 6ft 8in coupled wheels. Someone then had the bright idea of coupling a book about these Churchward designs of the first decade of the twentieth century with the similarly named but otherwise dissimilar Hawksworth 'Counties' built between 1945 and 1947. Perhaps they were not altogether dissimilar – the tender engines were both two-cylinder locomotives with Stephenson valve gear and – for their time – high pressure boilers. Designed perhaps more for cross-country duties on undulating railways rather than the Brunel 'billiard table' main line, they both acquired disappointing reputations, though for different reasons – the earlier 4-4-0s suffering from rough-riding and the 4-6-0s from indifferent steaming, at least until redraughting and fitting with double chimneys improved matters ten years after their construction.

Not having experienced the Churchward engines myself – they were all withdrawn four or five years before I was born – I have had to rely on research and photos from many other sources, although I do remember and have included some of my own experiences with the Hawksworth 4-6-0s. I am therefore grateful for the records from the *Railway Magazines* of the period from 1905 to 1929 which had occasional references to the 'County' 4-4-0s, especially in Cecil J Allen's 'British Locomotive Practice and Performance' articles and for the material in the 1977/8 David & Charles books on the Standard Gauge GW 4-4-0s written by O.S. Nock. The ever reliable RCTS publications on Great Western locomotives were a further valuable source of factual information. I am also indebted to John Hodge who gave me access to his unpublished magazine articles he had prepared on the 'County' 4-4-0s and 4-4-2Ts.

I am particularly grateful for being given access and permission to publish free of charge or at much reduced fee (as all the royalties as with earlier books are again being donated to the Railway Children charity) many photographs from the GW Trust archive at Didcot (Laurence Waters) and the Manchester Locomotive Society archive at Stockport station (Paul Shackcloth). Mike Bentley, a member of the MLS, has also being very generous in making his huge personal collection available to me and John Hodge has also helped and Dick Riley's friend, Rodney Lissenden and Dick's widow, Christine, have given me access to his collection of colour slides of the Hawksworth 'Counties' at work. I have endeavoured to trace and acknowledge all photos and their copyright owners, but if I have inadvertently missed anyone, please contact the publisher so I can put the matter right.

My thanks as ever to John Scott-Morgan, Pen & Sword's Commissioning Editor for the Transport Imprint for all his help, and particularly to Jodie Butterwood, Janet Brookes and Paul Wilkinson at Pen & Sword's Barnsley offices for their support and help. Finally, I am grateful for the knowledge and encouragement of my editor, Carol Trow, for her patience, and indeed expressed enthusiasm, for my work – undeserved but very flattering all the same!

David Maidment
September 2017

INTRODUCTION

This book covers the design, construction and operation of three classes of Great Western locomotives that were seen by many as comparative failures when compared with Churchward's other fleet of GW standard locomotives, or Collett's 'Kings' and 'Castles'. They were all short-lived compared with most other GW classes, the 'County' 4-4-0s and 'County Tanks' being displaced by more modern and suitable locomotives in the early 1930s, and the Hawksworth 'Counties' coming late in the day with their careers cut short by the rapid dieselisation of the Western Region between 1959 and 1965. However, as I will show, the 4-4-0s, despite their reputation as rough-riding engines, certainly had a turn of speed and took their place alongside the 'City' double-framed 4-4-0s with some distinction in the first decade of the twentieth century. It was just that the 4-4-0 design was found wanting in later years before and after the First World War as passenger travel increased and with it, train loads needing 4-6-0s. These engines may have compared poorly with other contemporary GW designs by Churchward, but I suggest that many other UK railway companies would have been glad of them.

The 4-4-2Ts were as rough-riding as their 4-4-0 sisters, it is alleged, though few records exist to confirm this. Their main drawback was the use of such large wheels for stopping suburban traffic and lack of adhesion with four instead of six coupled wheels. They would certainly have had a suitable turn of speed for longer distance semi-fast services from London to Oxford or Swindon, but as commuting increased and the London suburban services grew heavier, the 61XX 2-6-2 'Prairie Tanks' of 1931 outclassed them.

As for Hawksworth's 'Counties', many conjecture that the engineer really wanted to develop the GWR's second pacific class, but was constrained by wartime restrictions, and the 6ft 3in wheeled 280lbs pressure boilered engine was a compromise heralding greater things to come, which the 1948 nationalisation stifled. Their early work disappointed and their use on routes where they 'competed' with the long established 'Castles' did them no favours. Their concentration on routes where their power could be used in short bursts without draining the boiler and where they could get regular crews helped, and their equipment with double-chimneys after 1956 improved their steaming weakness but it was too late in the day, with the initial dieselisation aimed at the very routes where they were used at their best – Devon and Cornwall.

It is therefore useful to look in greater depth at these engines – two classes coincidentally both named after counties through which GW routes ran (or claimed to run!) and their tank engine equivalent. I will not hold back from criticism or whitewash some of the disappointments but attempt to give a balanced view of these locomotives that played useful roles in GW operations and income generation over the twenty to thirty years of their existence.

William Dean, who finally retired in 1902, was suffering from increasing mental health problems (a form of dementia) from the mid-1890s so his assistant, George Jackson Churchward, took increasing responsibilities for his designs, continuing to construct Dean's basic double-framed 4-4-0s, redesigned with his taper boiler developments. Churchward was preparing for office and in this interim period, was studying foreign locomotive design, especially in France and America and was impressed by the high-stepping American 4-4-0s and 4-4-2s with coned boilers and high running plate that were claiming a number of high speed performances at the time. He had produced his passenger 4-6-0 and freight 2-8-0 within the first year of becoming Locomotive Superintendent in name as well as practice, and despite being parallel with the construction of inside cylinder double-framed 4-4-0s, he designed and built a new outside cylinder single-framed 4-4-0 reflecting much of USA practice. Swindon Works continued to build further 4-4-0s in 1906 alongside the construction of the heavier 4-6-0s, and then surprisingly reverted to the double-framed 'Flower' class in 1908/9, before producing another batch of 'County' 4-4-0s in 1911/12.

It therefore would appear that despite their rough-riding experience compared with the 4-4-0 double-framed 'Cities', the design was useful enough to multiply as late as 1912, for at that stage the new 4-6-0s were only really in command of the prime West of England and Bristol routes, leaving the South Wales, Weymouth, Worcester and Birmingham line expresses in the hands of 4-4-0s until the end of the First World War.

Churchward created the 4-4-2Ts to replace the nineteenth century 2-4-0 'Metro Tanks' and the 1900 built 2-4-2T 3600 class which were proving inadequate on the developing London suburban services. It is perhaps surprising that he and the GW operating authorities did not recognise the prototype 2-6-2T No. 99 and the 31XX production engines as suitable for this type of work.

American E2 atlantic built in 1902 with tapered boiler and wide firebox. This engine was built as Pennsylvania Railroad No.8063, but was renumbered 7002 after a locomotive of the same class which was withdrawn in 1935 and was reputed to hold the world speed record for steam, claiming 127mph. However, the timing was unreliable, made by different observers in signalboxes three miles apart. What is known is that these engines and similar 4-4-0s were capable of speeds of around 100 mph, and Churchward would have studied them during his exposure to American locomotive practice at the turn of the century. The photo was taken at Northumberland, Pennsylvania, 9 August 1964. (MLS Collection)

1904 built 3480 *County of Stafford,* the boiler and cab sides 'guivered' (polished and decorated with tallow wax by cleaners usually at the request of the engine's regular driver), c1905. 3480 as built had a small copper-capped chimney and works plate on the saddle below the smokebox. (J.M. Bentley Collection/Real Photographs)

An early 'County' 4-4-0 in action, 3481 *County of Glamorgan,* with an up Bristol express between Acton and Old Oak Common, c1908. The engine is in original condition apart from the copper-cap chimney being replaced by a narrow cast-iron version. The North London line from Acton Yard to Willesden can be seen in the background. (GW Trust)

In their early years, they were seen as freight and banking engines and only later were seen to have the power and acceleration that fitted them for heavier stopping passenger trains than the 'County Tanks' could cope with. The author travelled behind a 6ft 8in 4-4-0 on an eight-coach London commuter service in 1958 (the preserved 3440 *City of Truro* was incongruously so used for about three months that summer on a morning Reading-Paddington turn and the 6.20pm Paddington-Reading in the evening) and with the packed train and a drizzly rainy evening, found great difficulty keeping its feet and maintaining time between stations, a problem that must have similarly afflicted the 4-4-2Ts in such conditions.

Charles Collett, succeeding Churchward, inherited an efficient locomotive fleet and – faced with pressures during the Depression years to cut costs – developed larger engines to Churchward's principles and improved the efficiency of Swindon Works and the economy of the maintenance regime throughout the system, without

One of the 1911 built 'Counties', 3821 *County of Bedford*, with the Holford inspired curved front to the footplating instead of the stark 'step', photographed shortly after the First World War outshopped in plain green livery with the copper cap on the slightly larger chimney painted over. The engine was built in superheated form and topfeed has been fitted. (GW Trust)

3824 *County* of Cornwall, built in December 1911, enters Shrewsbury with a stopping train from Hereford formed of a motley collection of vehicles, c1925. The front vehicle is a Churchward short wheelbase coach of the type used normally on the suburban service to Moorgate! (J.M. Bentley Collection/Photomatic)

1906 built 3803 *County Cork*, in its last year of life, departs Paddington with a stopping train for Reading, passing a new 61XX 2-6-2T that replaced them and their tank engine counterparts in the London area, and a 0-6-0PT engaged on ECS work, July 1931. Behind, just visible, is the electric Hammersmith & City stock (joint GW/ Metropolitan Railway). 3803 was withdrawn six months later. Although clearly rundown by this time, it sports a copper-cap chimney restored after postwar austerity and a small safety valve cover. (J.M. Bentley Collection/ Photomatic)

'County Tank' 2227 from the first batch built in 1906, with stepped front end and original straight bunker, but ex-works shortly after the First World War in plain green livery and copper cap chimney painted over. (MLS Collection/F. Moore postcard)

1906 built 2224 with cast-iron chimney and extended bunker heads an eight-coach Paddington-Reading stopping train (for which these engines were less than ideal) past Kensal Green gasworks in the mid-1920s. Note that the engine has no lamp bracket on the smokebox, so the lamp is positioned on the centre of the bufferbeam. (GW Trust)

any further dramatic creative or development initiatives of his own.

When he retired in 1941, handing over the reins to Frederick Hawksworth, a CME in waiting then already fifty-seven years of age, the latter had little choice but to balance the need for the Works to become heavily involved in munitions production as decreed by the Board and look elsewhere for help with the massive freight requirement that developed during the war. He was able to continue the build of the 2-8-0s, now in the 3800 series and met the Ministry of Transport demand to use Swindon's facilities to build the Stanier 8Fs, a design chosen for the international role that the Dean Goods 0-6-0s and the Robinson RODs had undertaken in the First World War.

In the immediate aftermath of the war, faced with increasing coal shortages, Hawksworth initiated a substantial oil-burning conversion programme, but had to close it after only two years when the British Government suffered a balance of payments problem that made it impossible to secure the fuel required. Hawksworth had to wait until after the war before he could initiate any of his own design ideas, and, apart the successful 'Modified Halls' and a couple of classes of pannier tanks, he was not required to develop any new freight designs. He could therefore, at last, turn to the possibility of a large passenger locomotive design.

As hinted earlier, the genesis of his 'County' seems to have been the intention to create a GW pacific locomotive with high boiler pressure (after the example of Bulleid's 'Merchant Navies') and 6ft 3in coupled wheels creating a

locomotive theoretically of very significant power. Limitations of build during and in the immediate aftermath of the Second World War meant that Hawksworth identified his new passenger engine as a mixed traffic 6MT (as classified later after nationalisation). Perhaps a mistake was made in allocating the initial batch to Old Oak Common and Bristol Bath Road in 1946/7 and using them on prestige services on the level mainline where continuous steaming was necessary and the 'Castles' excelled, rather than on more heavily graded routes where their theoretical power could be required for maximum output for relatively short periods. Hawksworth was defensive about his creations but he must have been disappointed to find that they were soon relegated from the GW/WR's

most important expresses, except the *Cornish Riviera* and *Cornishman* west of Plymouth. Hawksworth remained as CME throughout the formation of the Western Region of British Railways in 1948, retiring in late 1949, and dying aged ninety-two in 1976.

1009 *County of Carmarthen* was tested with a redraughted double-chimney (an ugly steel stovepipe at first) in 1954 and from 1956 the results led to new rather squat double-chimneys being fitted to all the 'Counties' up until 1959, although their improved usefulness was limited by the impending dieselisation with the 'Warship' hydraulic fleet under construction from 1958. No further major repairs took place after 1961/2 and the last one, 1011 *County of Chester*, was withdrawn in November 1964.

1000 *County of Middlesex* as built with large double chimney (which proved no more effective than the production run single chimneys) shortly after naming in March 1946. (GW Trust)

1019 *County* of *Merioneth* running in on a Swindon-Didcot local train at Swindon shortly after being constructed and named in April 1946. 1019 has the standard single chimney and the final GWR livery for passenger locomotives. (MLS Collection/ H.C. Casserley)

1025 *County* of Radnor at its home depot, Shrewsbury, after being fitted with the new style low double chimney in August 1959. 1025 spent most of its life working between Wolverhampton, Shrewsbury and Chester. (MLS Collection/J. Davenport)

Double chimney 'County' 1006 *County of Cornwall* on the down *Cornishman* from the Midlands, entering Truro station, 20 May 1959. (G.W. Trust/M. Mensing)

Chapter 1

CHURCHWARD'S COUNTY 4-4-0S

The first of the class, 3473 *County of Middlesex*, at Swindon shortly after construction, 1904. (J.M. Bentley Collection)

Design & Construction

Churchward had been content to develop Dean's double-framed 4-4-0s for the Great Western Railway's express passenger traffic at the turn of the century, using the basic design to experiment with his boiler improvements, whilst setting out his stall for standardisation of the GW locomotive fleet to be implemented once he had taken over the reins fully in 1902. Whilst the key needs were for a more powerful express engine for the increasing traffic – his 4-6-0s – and a 2-8-0 for the company's profitable coal traffic, the range of designs he submitted to the GW Board included a 4-4-0 for secondary and cross-country duties, and constructed from the standard parts that would be incorporated in his other new designs.

Some argued that the LNWR civil engineer's prohibition of the proposed 4-6-0 on the jointly managed North & West route between Shrewsbury and Hereford was the main 'raison d'être' for the standard outside cylindered 4-4-0, but there were other routes

3479 *County* of *Warwick* on royal train duty in the month of its construction, October 1904.

Note the simplified livery on the tender, the royal coat of arms and royal 'crown' headlamp, also the loco is fitted with a small copper-cap chimney.
(MLS/Bob Miller Collection)

3476 *County* of *Dorset* at Old Oak Common shortly after the depot's opening, c1907. The locomotive now bears another simplified livery with the GW crest on the tender between the words 'Great Western'. It is still fitted with the original small copper cap chimney although many were receiving narrow cast-iron chimneys by this time. (GW Trust)

where length restrictions applied (for example, because of short turntables) or loads did not justify the expense of a 4-6-0. Having successfully demonstrated the 4-6-0, 2-8-0 and 2-6-2T prototypes, ten 4-4-0s with conventional inside frames and two outside cylinders emerged from Swindon Works in 1904 around the same time as his double-framed 'Cities' were making their remarkable debut on the Plymouth-London Ocean Mails. They were numbered 3473-3482 consecutively after the latest range of double-framed 4-4-0s and were named after counties served by the company.

Their key dimensions, in accord with Churchward's new standards, included two large 18in x 30in outside cylinders, coupled wheels of 6ft 8½in diameter, bogie wheels 3ft 2in, Stephenson valve gear, boiler pressure of 200lbs psi, grate area 20.56sqft and total heating surface of 1,818.12sqft. Total length of the engine (excluding tender) was just 24ft, and weight was 55 tons 6 cwt plus a 3,000 gallon capacity 36 ton 15 cwt tender, making the total weight 92 tons 1 cwt. Axle-load at just over 18 tons was significantly heavier than the double-framed engines, but the engine packed a punch with tractive effort (at 85%) of well over 20,000lbs. They sported small copper-capped chimneys and tall safety valve bonnets on the domeless tapered No.4 boiler, and had square steps to the running plate at the front over the cylinders,

as for his 4-6-0s. Accused at the time by enthusiasts of being stark, ugly engines after the American fashion, so unlike Dean's elegant engines with their flowing curves, we now look back on them as compact neat engines, simple and straightforward. The names of the initial ten 1904 built locomotives were:

3473	*County of Middlesex*
3474	*County of Berks*
3475	*County of Wilts*
3476	*County of Dorset*
3477	*County of Somerset*
3478	*County of Devon*
3479	*County of Warwick*
3480	*County of Stafford*
3481	*County of Glamorgan*
3482	*County of Pembroke*

3476 stands at Reading at the head of an up express, c 1908. It has received the new simplified livery with GW crest between the company's name and has exchanged its copper cap chimney for a narrow cast-iron one.
(MLS/Bob Miller Collection/ Loco & General Company)

Another photo of 3479 *County of Warwick* standing ready to take up royal train duties, October 1904. (GW Trust)

A portrait of 3477 *County of Somerset* with the original livery, lined with the elaborate GWR scroll, shortly after construction in August 1904. 3477 (as 3834 after 1912) was the last survivor of the class, withdrawn in November 1933, having run just over a million miles in traffic. The cab and tender have been 'guivered' by the cleaners (with tallow wax, a practice demanded by some drivers to distinguish their 'own' engines). J.M. Bentley Collection/Loco & General photos

3480 *County* of *Stafford* on Shrewsbury shed with a 'City' double-framed 4-4-0, c 1905. 3480 has also received special attention from the cleaners 'guivering' the boiler and cab side. (GW Trust)

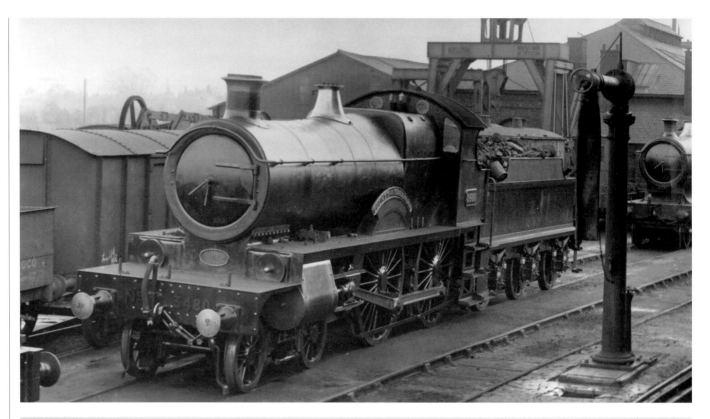

3479 *County* of *Warwick* on shed at Swindon with its simplified livery, c1906. Two Dean 'Singles' are in the background. (MLS/Bob Miller Collection/ Loco Publishing Company)

The GW became logical and systematic in its naming policy, but in this instance the omission of Buckinghamshire and Cornwall on the GW's main route to the West Country was surprising although put right in later builds (and followed scrupulously for the Hawksworth 'Counties' later). To undermine the rumour that they had been built to meet the LNWR's stipulations for the North & West, none of these ten were specifically allocated there, all going to supplement the 'Cities' at Paddington, Newton Abbot and Bristol, and share in the main West of England traffic until more 4-6-0s were available. Despite the fact that these engines soon developed a reputation for rough-riding, they were deemed successful enough for a further twenty to be built in 1906, the first ten of which were named after counties in Ireland as the GW was keen to expand and publicise its Irish Sea ferry traffic to Rosslare and Southern Ireland. These next ten were therefore named:

3801	*County Carlow*
3802	*County Clare*
3803	*County Cork*
3804	*County Dublin*
3805	*County Kerry*
3806	*County Kildare*
3807	*County Kilkenny*
3808	*County Limerick*
3809	*County Wexford*
3810	*County Wicklow*

These engines appeared in Churchward's new simplified livery with black frames and cylinders in place of the previous Indian red, and the elaborate scroll on the tender being replaced by the company's garter crest in between the wording 'Great ......Western'. It is apparent that Churchward was much more interested in the performance of his new engines than their external appearance and it was the persuasion of others that retained the GW trademark copper-capped chimney, brass and later softened the stark outline of his engines with curves in some of the right places!

The last ten engines of this batch reverted to English and Welsh

3809 *County Wexford* delivered new in 1906 and seen here c1908 posing with staff from its allocated depot, Old Oak Common. It has a larger chimney but the copper cap is painted over and the tender livery has been further simplified with the removal of the GW crest. It still has tall safety valve cover but has topfeed. (GW Trust)

3803 *County* Cork, ex works from Swindon with short safety valve cover and topfeed, c1910. Sister locomotive 3805 *County Kerry* is featured in the background. 3803 is now fitted with a larger standard GW copper cap chimney.
(J.M. Bentley Collection/Real Photos)

counties repairing the omission of 'Bucks' but surprisingly still omitting obvious counties in GW territory such as Cornwall and Gloucestershire whilst introducing obscure GW claims to Leicestershire and Hampshire. One wonders if any public relations politics were at work here or whether someone's geographical knowledge was a little lacking:

3811 *County of Bucks*
3812 *County of Cardigan*
3813 *County of Carmarthen*
3814 *County of Cheshire* (renamed *County of Chester* May 1907)
3815 *County of Hants*
3816 *County of Leicester*
3817 *County of Monmouth*
3818 *County of Radnor*
3819 *County of Salop*
3820 *County of Worcester.*

There were some other detail differences in the design of these twenty engines. They had cast-iron chimneys, vacuum instead of steam brake and 3,500 gallon tenders weighing 40 tons.

The cast-iron chimneys were replaced by larger copper-capped chimneys in 1907. One locomotive, 3805, was equipped in 1907 with a lighter No.2 boiler, reducing the heating surface to 1,517.89sqft, grate area to 20.35sqft, 195lbs psi boiler pressure and tractive effort to almost exactly 20,000lbs.There is some inconsistency in GW records here as the lighter boiler should have reduced its weight by around 3½ tons, but in fact it was recorded as weighting 58 tons 10 cwt, 3½ tons heavier, with an increased axle-weight of 19 tons 4 cwt. One assumes there is an error in the records for this or the standard engines, for presumably the experiment was intended to lessen the track hammer blow or improve the riding of the engine. Whatever the reason, it was insufficient to be worth changing other locomotives and a No.4 boiler was restored to 3805 in May 1909 (for photo of 3805 with No.2 boiler in action, see page 43).

3818 *County of Radnor* built in December 1906 photographed in Works Grey. Note fitted with narrow cast iron chimney and tall safety valve cover without topfeed.
(GW Trust/ British Railways)

3813 *County of Carmarthen* built in 1906, seen here a few years later but before the First World War, its narrow cast-iron chimney replaced by a large copper cap chimney and topfeed, though still with tall safety valve cover.
(MLS Collection/F Moore)

3819 *County* of *Salop* at Swindon around the time of the start of the First World War, equipped with copper cap chimney and tall safety valve cover with topfeed.
(GW Trust)

Superheating of these locomotives began in 1909 with 3477 and 3804 and proceeded apace in 1910, before a further batch of ten, numbered 3821-3830 was built in 1911-12. These were built with superheaters and topfeed and also screw, as opposed to lever, reverse and curved footplating in front of the cylinders and under the cab. Smokeboxes of all the engines were lengthened by nine inches. These later engines were also recorded as weighing 58 tons 16 cwt plus a 40 ton 3,500 gallon tender which casts

some doubt on the quoted weight of 55 tons for the 3473-82 series. The new batch of locomotives were named as under:

3821	*County of Bedford*
3822	*County of Brecon*
3823	*County of Carnarvon*
3824	*County of Cornwall*
3825	*County of Denbigh*
3826	*County of Flint*
3827	*County of Gloucester*
3828	*County of Hereford*
3829	*County of Merioneth*
3830	*County of Oxford*

'Cornwall' made its belated appearance and I am not quite sure which bit of Bedfordshire the GW claimed and 'Flint' was pushing its incursion into LNWR territory to the limit. In the general renumbering in December 1912, the 3473-3482 series were brought into line with the rest of the 'Counties' which retained their 38XX numbers, the prototype 3473 fittingly assuming the mantle of the vacant 3800, the other older engines tagging on behind as 3831-3839.

Few other changes were made during the remaining twenty or so years of the class's life. In true GW style, parts were interchangeable so boilers were exchanged. Some engines carried cast-iron chimneys again, and appeared on different locomotives as boilers were swapped. ATC was fitted to some engines very early after its invention (3803/04/07/09 in 1908) and all except 3831/32 had been equipped by February 1931, after some of the class had already been withdrawn.

A few also had the shorter safety valve bonnets. The redundant eight-wheel bogie tender from the GW pacific, *The Great Bear*, converted to a 'Castle' in 1924, was linked to 'County' 3804, then later paired with 3802 and 3816 after works overhauls.

The first engine of the 1912 'lot', 3821 *County of Bedford*, with curved footplating in front of cylinders and under the cab, in Works Grey as built in 1912.
(GW Trust/British Railways)

The new 3828 *County of Hereford* with modified footplating, with 1906 built 3812 *County of Cardigan* behind, Swindon, 1912. (GW Trust)

3825 *County of Denbigh* built in December 1911 at an unidentified shed with a 'Bulldog' and a 43XX mogul, in full lined prewar livery, c1913. (GW Trust)

3832 (former 1904 engine 3475) *County of Wilts* at Old Oak Common in the post First World War plain green livery. (GW Trust)

3838 (numbered 3481 when built in 1904) *County of Glamorgan* at Old Oak Common, in GW plain green livery and painted over copper cap chimney, 29.4.1922. It is the stated longterm intention of the Great Western Society to reconstruct a replica of this locomotive from many GW standard parts that still exist. (GW Trust)

The second 'County' to receive the eight-wheel bogie tender that had been coupled to 111 *The Great Bear* before its conversion to a 'Castle' in 1924, then allocated to 3804, and subsequently to 3802 *County Clare*, c 1927. (GW Trust)

3816 *County of Leicester* attached to *The Great Bear* eight-wheel bogie tender, first 3804, then 3802 and finally 3816, at Old Oak Common, c1929. (GW Trust)

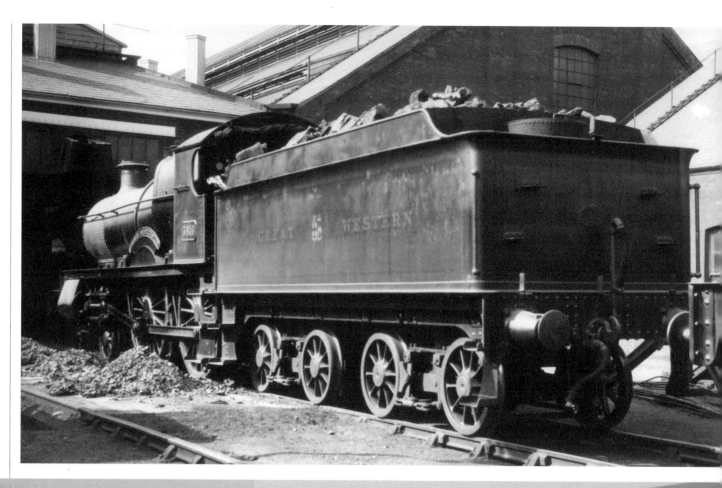

3816 *County of Leicester* with the bogie tender from *The Great Bear* at Swindon on a stopping train to Bristol, 25 May 1931. (J.M. Bentley Collection)

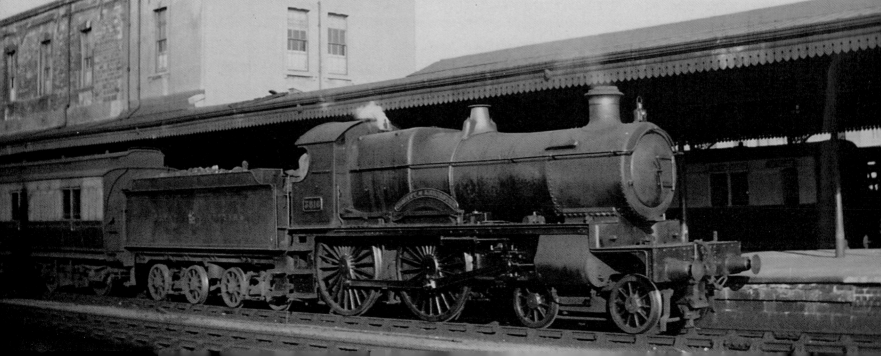

The prototype 3473 *County of Middlesex*, renumbered 3800 in 1912 as the 'class leader' seen here in the 1920s. (GW Trust)

In the immediate aftermath of the First World War the 'Counties' were painted a plain green with the copper cap chimney painted over. Later some lining was restored together with the GW crest/coat of arms between the words 'Great ….Western' on the tender. In general usage on secondary services, the pristine condition of the engines suffered, especially in the latter part of the decade before withdrawal in the early 1930s.

3805 *County* Kerry at Oxford in the early 1920s. (GW Trust)

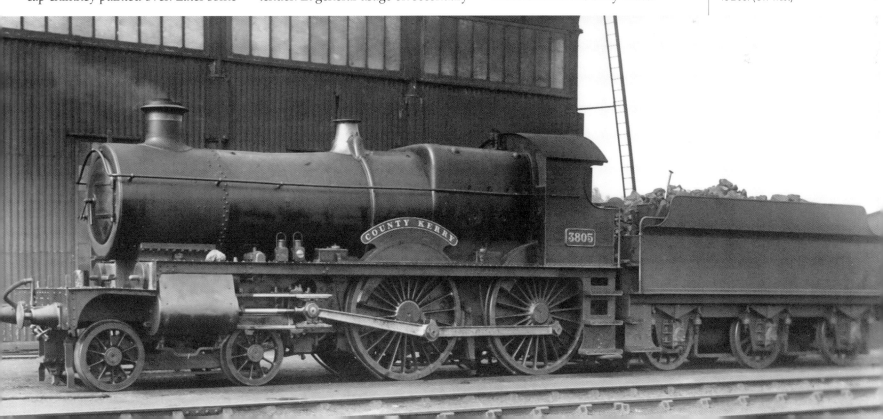

3812 *County* of *Cardigan* in the early 1920s.
(GW Trust)

3825 *County* of *Denbigh* in plain green livery and cast-iron chimney at Ranelagh Bridge, Paddington, in the early 1920s.
(MLS Collection/F Moore)

The last days – photos of the 'Counties' on shed in the last two or three years of their operation.

3801 *County* Carlow at Shrewsbury, c1929.
(J.M. Bentley Collection/ Photmatic)

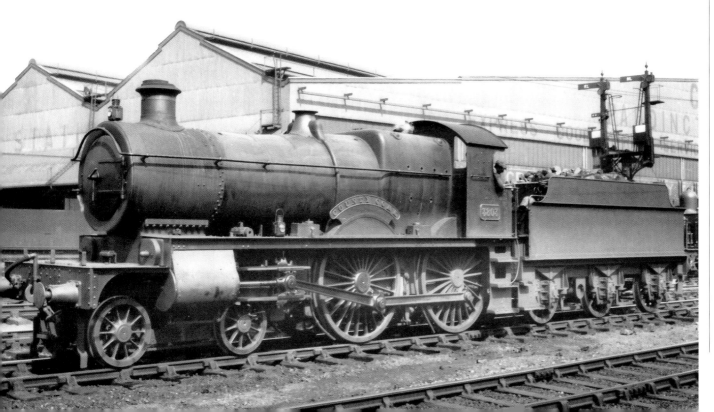

3803 *County* Cork at Paddington, August 1931.
(J.M. Bentley Collection/ Photmatic)

3810 *County* Wicklow after a 'casual' Works repair (note smokebox only repainted).
(J.M. Bentley Collection/Real Photographs)

3814 *County* of Chester at Reading shed, c1932.
(GW Trust)

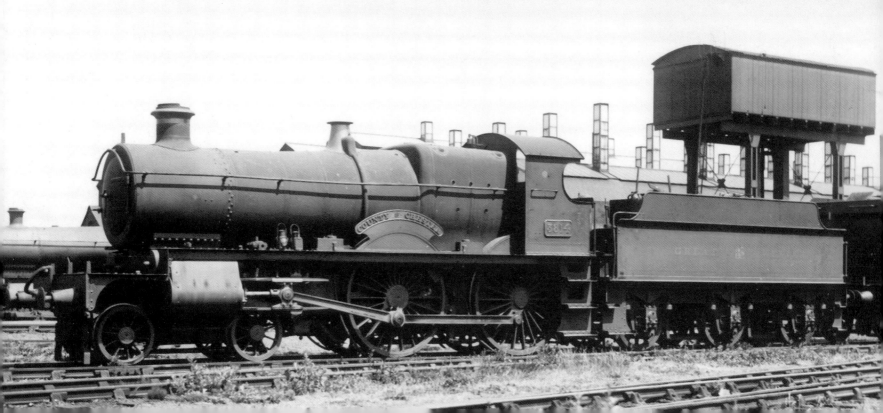

3820 *County of Worcester*, c 1931 with Collett 0-6-0 2259 built in 1930 in the background.
(MLS Collection/F. Moore)

3825 *County* of Denbigh at Oxford, 9 April 1927.
(J.M. Bentley Collection/H.C. Casserley)

3828 *County* of
Hereford and a 63XX
mogul at Reading, c1930.
(GW Trust)

3834 *County* of *Somerset*
(formerly 3477) at Old
Oak Common, c1930.
(J.M. Bentley Collection)

3836 *County of Warwick* (formerly 3479), c1930. (GW Trust)

3833, built in 1904, was the first to be condemned in February 1930. Withdrawals then took place steadily until the last one – also a 1904 survivor, 3834 , the former

3477 – was taken out of service in November 1933, rendering the class extinct. It is reported that the GW Society at Didcot has long term plans to build a new

'County' 4-4-0 including some existing standard parts not needed for other preservation projects, but in 2016 this is seen as a far-off dream.

One of the last four surviving 'County' 4-4-0s, 3828 *County of Hereford*, at Reading shed just a couple of months before withdrawal in March 1933. It looks in remarkably good condition for an engine so near the scrap yard. (J.M. Bentley Collection)

3814 *County of Chester*, withdrawn in June 1931, stored at the Swindon Dump, awaiting scrapping in 1933.
(J.M. Bentley Collection/Real Photographs)

3820 *County of Worcester* with 2-4-2T 3620 awaiting scrapping at the Swindon Dump, 25 May 1931.
(J.M. Bentley Collection)

Operation

Sir William Stanier once reported in a discussion at the Institution of Locomotive Engineers in 1950 that Churchward designed the 4-4-0 'Counties' specifically for the jointly owned Shrewsbury-Hereford route for which the LNWR had the infrastructure responsibility and the GWR covered motive power. As the LNWR civil engineer forbade Churchward's 4-6-0s, he created a 4-4-0 version of them, which perversely delivered an even heavier hammer-blow to the other company's track – 8 tons per six revolutions compared with 6.4 tons for 'Saint' and just 3.6 tons for an inside cylinder 4-4-0 (and only 1.9 tons for a four-cylinder 'Star'). However, if that had been the plan, one would have expected the new engines to have been allocated to the North & West sheds like Shrewsbury and Pontypool from the start. Of the first ten built in 1904, six were allocated to the London depot at Westbourne Park and one to Newton Abbot, with only three at Bristol Bath Road from where they could work south or east as well as to Shrewsbury.

The second batch of twenty locomotives, 3801-3820, built in 1906, were similarly allocated over the prime routes of the GWR, with eight at the new depot at Old Oak Common, six to South Wales (five to Cardiff Canton and one to Swansea Landore), one to Exeter, two to Wolverhampton Stafford Road, a further two to Bristol Bath Road and finally two to Shrewsbury, the first, 3814, in November 1906. The third batch of ten, 3821-3830, in 1911-12, was mainly drafted to Wolverhampton with another two to Bristol and lastly, one to Swindon.

In service with piston valves and 6¼in valve travel plus Stephenson link motion they were good starters despite being 4-4-0s, but soon acquired a reputation for rough-riding compared to the 'Cities' and other inside cylinder 4-4-0s. K.J. Cook blamed the hammering of the left-hand trailing axleboxes and the short rigid wheelbase. Interestingly, some other contemporary 4-4-0s had even heavier axleloads and hammer blow – for instance the superheated Caledonian Dunalistair, the SECR 'L', the NER 'R' (later LNER D20) or the LNWR 'George V'. However, both the 'L' and the 'R' were good riding engines despite the stresses created on the track.

The prototype, 3473, was subject to a number of dynamometer tests at the back end of 1904 with an eleven-coach train of 260 tons, with ¼ open regulator and 25% cut-off, and ¾ regulator and 15% cut-off, both at 60mph on the level giving drawbar pulls of 1.6 and 1.3 tons respectively. On the slightly rising gradient between Didcot and Swindon, with 18% cut-off and speed between 58 and 62mph, drawbar horsepower of 665 was achieved (compared to 1,100hp with a 4-6-0 with higher boiler pressure).

3473 *County* of *Middlesex* at Bristol Temple Meads running in on a stopping train to Swindon, 1904. (GW Trust)

3474 *County* of *Berks* piloting an 'Atbara' 4-4-0 at Whiteball on a West of England express, 1904. (J.M. Bentley Collection)

A Dean 'Single' 4-2-2 pilots 3480 *County of Stafford* on a Shrewsbury-London train at an unknown location, c1907. (GW Trust)

Initially they shared main line work from London to Bristol and the West Country with the 'Atbaras' and 'Cities'. Rous-Marten timed 3479 *County of Warwick* on a 295 ton train between Bristol and Exeter in 1905 which initially ran in the low 60s as far as Worle Junction but a side gale off the Severn Estuary affected the running badly until Taunton was reached, from where a good climb to Whiteball was made without falling below 30mph. A better run was made in the up direction with 3474 *County of Berks* and a 305 gross ton train which made a vigorous start to Whiteball, averaging 46.2 mph from Tiverton Junction, falling to 38½mph at the summit (a slight easing after Burlescombe, possibly due to a drop in steam pressure) followed by a swift descent in the upper 70s. After a bad p-way slack near Bridgwater, speed recovered to nearly 70mph after Flax Bourton and Bedminster was passed in 74 minutes net for the 74.5 miles.

The train was non-stop to London and despite signal checks at Didcot, Maidenhead and before Southall, arrival was slightly early in an actual time of 169 minutes 40 seconds from passing Taunton at speed (162.8 miles) and a net time of 197 minutes for the 193.6 miles from Exeter. Dauntsey was cleared at 47½mph and speed ranged between 65 and 70mph from Swindon to the Didcot check and was steady at 66mph through Reading, before another check at Maidenhead.

3477 *County* of *Somerset* accelerates through Warminster on a Cardiff-Salisbury-Portsmouth express, c1908.
(GW Trust)

3478 *County of Devon* hurries a down express past Hayes, c1908. (GW Trust)

3478 *County* of Devon assists an Armstrong 0-6-0 (rebuild of a 2-2-2 passenger engine) on an up coal train between Badminton and Swindon, c1908. (GW Trust)

3817 *County* of *Monmouth* and **3477 *County of Somerset*** at Swindon on excursions to visit the Works on an 'Open Day', c1907. (J.M. Bentley Collection)

A run around the same period timed by A.V. Goodyear with 3479 and 228/245 tons accelerated vigorously after a p-way restriction at Cowley Bridge Junction, achieved 66mph at Collumpton, minimum of 41mph at Whiteball but another p-way slack spoilt the descent through Wellington.

Despite a signal stop outside Bristol, Temple Meads was reached over two minutes early on a schedule of 86 minutes for the 75.6 miles (net time approximately 76 minutes). R.E. Charlewood experienced an exceptionally heavy thirteen-coach 400 ton gross train from Plymouth with

3481 *County of Glamorgan* which stopped at Swindon and ran from Shrivenham to Reading (35.5 miles) in 33 minutes 56 seconds, and despite checks east of Reading completed a stop at Ealing Broadway (71.6 miles) in just over 77 minutes (74 net) at an average speed of 58mph.

3814 *County of Chester* on the 12.30pm Shrewsbury-Paddington at an unidentified location, 28 February 1907.
(GW Trust)

3805 *County Kerry*, the lone example fitted with a Swindon Standard No.2 boiler, passes Acton with an up parcels and milk train, 1908. The boiler was replaced by a Standard No.4 boiler the following year restoring it to similar condition to the rest of the class.
(GW Trust)

3814 *County* of *Chester* at No.2 platform at Paddington with a Birmingham express, c1910.
(J.M. Bentley/Photomatic)

3814 *County* of *Chester* at Bentley Heath with a Birmingham-Paddington express, 1911.
(GW Trust)

3807 *County* *Kilkenny* passes Acton on an up West of England express, c1912.
(MLS Collection)

3817 *County* *of Monmouth* at Patchway with an LNWR/ Shrewsbury-Bristol express, c 1910.
(GW Trust)

3816 *County* of *Leicester* with 0-6-0 saddle tank No.1978 at Weymouth, c1912.
(GW Trust)

3817 *County* of *Monmouth* climbs Filton Bank near Ashley Hill with a Bristol-Shrewsbury express, c1912.
(GW Trust)

3801 *County Carlow* with an up South Wales express at Hayes, c1920. (GW Trust)

However, they were soon displaced by the new 4-6-0s, and were found subsequently on trains to South Wales, Weymouth and Worcester. The 1911-12 batch based at Stafford Road worked the lightweight expresses to London via the newly opened Bicester route in competition with the LNWR. A few did work on the North & West, but eventually the LNWR track authorities gave way and allowed the 29XX 'Saints' to operate over the line during the First World War and they become the main motive power in the 1920s on both the South Wales-London trains and the North & West.

The first record of a 'County' on the North & West was a run in August 1909 from Chester to Bristol with 3814, which was timed from Shrewsbury by Rev. W.A. Dunn. The train had twelve coaches of mixed LNWR/GWR stock, 300 tons tare, and passed Church Stretton in 23 minutes 41 seconds, with 31mph up the initial 1 in 127, 48mph after Condover and a minimum of 28mph on the 1 in 100 past Leebotwood. Maximum speed was 75mph in the descent from Marshbrook to Craven Arms and the 63 minute schedule for the 51 miles was well in hand before catching up a slower train ahead at Leominster. The 33.5 miles from Hereford to Pontypool Road took 46 minutes 10 seconds – a

very creditable time – regaining three minutes lost before Hereford from the Leominster check, but then time was lost with a series of checks from Severn Tunnel Junction to Bristol.

A run on the Worcester route was logged on 21 December 1906 with newly built 3804 *County Dublin* on the 1.40pm from Paddington with a heavy 14-coach load of 342/375 tons, reduced to 267/285 after slipping four vehicles at Kingham. The start to Southall was slow, taking nearly 15 minutes but the 4-4-0 averaged nearly 60mph from Slough to Culham with sustained 62-64mph before Reading and the upper 50s after Reading. However, a bad p-way slack over Nuneham Bridge before Oxford caused the train to take 73 minutes to clear Oxford, four minutes late. It averaged nearly 55mph before the Kingham slowing to slip the coaches, then with 69mph down Honeybourne bank, and a steady 65-66mph in from Evesham, Worcester was reached on time in 134 minutes 50 seconds (or about 130 minutes net for the 120.4 miles).

Until 1910, GW London-Birmingham trains were routed via Oxford and this was a service that the new 'Counties' shared with other 4-4-0s. 3473 *County of Middlesex* with 220 tons was badly delayed by both p-way and signal checks before Reading,

and suffered another p-way slack near Appleford, passing Oxford in 67 minutes 30 seconds, but then ran vigorously covering the 22.7 miles to Banbury in 21 minutes 35 seconds (top speed 66 mph at Kings Sutton) and the 19.8 miles on to the Leamington stop in 20 minutes 35 seconds – timed from the slip coach. Arrival was nearly seven minutes late entirely due to the delays early in the run. 3804 *County Dublin* was also delayed by a severe p-way check between Slough and Maidenhead and averaged 64mph between Reading and Didcot and again between Radley and Oxford but was slightly slower than 3473 onwards and was checked again by p-way

work near Harbury spoiling the descent to Leamington where the slip coach arrived 1½ minutes late. An even better run was timed by R.E. Charlewood with 3479 *County of Warwick* with 200 tons when Reading was passed in 36 minutes, averaging 67mph from Slough, and Oxford in just over 63 minute despite a signal check at Tilehurst. Time was in hand to cover two moderate p-way slacks at Culham and Aynho and 75 mph was touched at Southam Road before a slow approach to Leamington as it was necessary to stop to detach the slip coach on this occasion. Actual time was 109 minutes 9 seconds for the 106 miles, but the net time was only 103 minutes.

3819 *County of Salop* on a Birmingham-Paddington express c1910.
(GW Trust)

3831 *County* of *Berks* at Birmingham Snow Hill with an express for Paddington, immediately after renumbering from 3474 in December 1912. (J.M. Bentley Collection)

3837 *County* of *Stafford* (ex 3480) on the 12.30pm Paddington-Birmingham at Bentley Heath, 12 June 1913. (GW Trust)

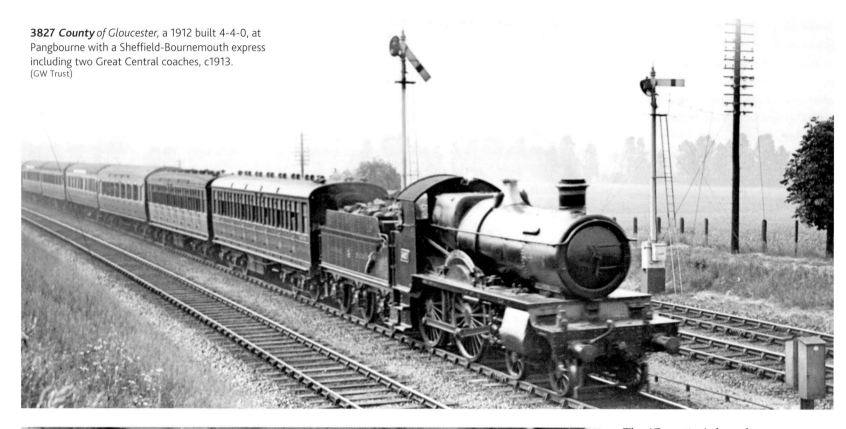

3827 *County of Gloucester*, a 1912 built 4-4-0, at Pangbourne with a Sheffield-Bournemouth express including two Great Central coaches, c1913.
(GW Trust)

3832 *County of Wilts* at Paddington platform 2 with a down Bristol train and a 'Star' on a West of England train on platform 1, c1913.
(GW Trust)

The 'Counties' shared express work on the Bristol road at this time, including the fast two-hour trains, although they seem to have had little in hand when the loads approached 300 tons on these popular services. An up run in 1907 with 3802 *County Clare* and 295 tons gross dropped four minutes to Didcot unchecked, despite clearing Badminton at 50mph, averaging 71.6 down the bank, suggesting a top speed of over 75mph and sustaining 66-68mph on to Didcot passed in 70 minutes 25 seconds for the 64.5 miles. Signal checks before Reading, Slough and Southall put paid to any time recovery and arrival was six minutes late, the net time around the scheduled two hours. There were, however, two examples of fast running by the same engine, 3820 *County of Worcester*, on the West of England route in 1907 when the 4-6-0s had taken over the main services. On the first, 3820 took over in an emergency at Exeter after 4-6-0 2908 failed with a hot box, and ran the 190ton train to London over the Castle Cary 173.7 mile route in 177 minutes 20 seconds with excellent work between Taunton and Westbury after initial delays, averaging over 60mph on the adverse gradients between these points. On the second run, also in 1907, 3820 surprisingly had command of the *Cornish Riviera Express* all the way from Plymouth and ran the heavier 290 ton load non-stop from Exeter to Paddington in just ten seconds over the three-hour schedule.

3836 *County* of Warwick (ex 3479) at Paddington platform 1 with a down express, c1914.
(GW Trust)

3830 *County* of Oxford, the last County to be built in December 1912, on an express made up of coaches in the short-lived GW chocolate lake livery, at Leamington Spa on a down express for Birmingham, c1914.
(GW Trust)

3836 *County* of *Warwick* (ex 3479) at speed with a down London-Bristol express somewhere between Southall and Slough, c1914.
(GW Trust)

3821 *County* of *Bedford* built in 1912 running along the sea wall into Teignmouth on a down express, c1914.
(J.M. Bentley Collection)

In the last years before the First World War, the 'Counties' were the regular steeds for the Bristol-Birmingham via Honeybourne services and four runs were quoted by O.S. Nock in the second part of his books on the GW 4-4-0s (David & Charles, 1978).

Bristol Stapleton Road – Cheltenham – Stratford – Birmingham, 1909 - 1914

Distance/Location	3812 County of Cardigan 175 tons		3800 County of Middlesex 175 tons		3837 County of Stafford 180 tons		3828 County of Hereford 295 tons	
Miles	Times Speed Mins secs		Times Speed Mins secs		Times Speed Mins secs		Times Speed Mins secs	
0.0 Bristol Stapleton Rd	00.00		00.00		00.00		00.00	
3.2 Filton	07.30		08.05		07.45		09.25 sigs	
10.3 Yate	18.45		20.15		20.00		22.35	
17.0 Charfield	25.15		26.40		27.00		30.45	
24.6 Coaley	33.05	58.1 ave	33.20	68.5 ave	33.25	75/71	37.15	62.8 ave
30.1 Standish Jcn	39.45		39.10		38.40		42.40	
37.4 Engine Shed Jcn	48.30 sigs		49.15 sigs		-	sigs	50.25	
43.1 Cheltenham	56.35		57.25		57.35		58.45	1 E
0.0	00.00		00.00		00.00		00.00	
5.6 Gotherington	08.35		08.35		-		09.55	
9.0 Winchcombe	12.30		12.40		11.35		14.15	
16.1 Broadway	20.55	pws	19.25		17.35		21.00	
21.1 Honeybourne E Jcn	25.25	66.8 ave	23.55	66.8 ave	22.30	63.3 ave	25.35	65.7 ave
26.1 Milcote	29.55		28.35		-		30.10	
29.1 Stratford-on-Avon	33.15	1 ¾ E	31.55	3 E	31.40	3 ¼ E	33.35	1½ E
							00.00	
8.0 Henley-in-Arden							11.10	
14.8 Earlswood Lakes							19.30	48.7 ave
21.7 Tyseley							26.50	
25.0 Birmingham S.H.							32.10	

A further run with 3806 *County Kildare* was timed just between Stratford and Birmingham with an even heavier load of 305 tons gross, and after a slower start, averaged 50.3mph up the long 1 in 150 to Earlswood Lakes, taking 33 minutes 25 seconds overall after a signal check before destination (net 32 minutes).

After the Bicester route to Birmingham opened, although 4-6-0s were rostered for the heavier trains, most of the lighter expresses were diagrammed for 4-4-0s, especially the 'Flowers' and the 'Counties'. Cecil J Allen published a number of runs on the heavy 9.10am Paddington-Birmingham two-hour train which included a stop at High Wycombe. Five runs in 1911 were with 4-6-0s with tonnages between 200 and 280, but he included two runs when 'Counties' were substituted with 275 and 310 tons and both kept the two hour schedule. The locomotives were 3830 *County of Oxford* and 3801

County Carlow, and struggled – as did the 4-6-0s – to keep the tight 30 minute schedule for the 26.5 miles to High Wycombe, losing one and two minutes respectively. Both trains slipped coaches at Bicester, Banbury and Leamington and achieved net times of 86¾ (3830) and 85 minutes (3801) for the 84.1 miles from High Wycombe to Birmingham , each arriving a minute early. *County Carlow* with the heavier load topped Saunderton at 45½mph, touched 80½mph at Haddenham, 55mph minimum at Ardley and 82 after Southam Road just before the Leamington slowing, and then mounted Hatton bank at a minimum of 53mph, although by this time the load had reduced to 160 tons after further coaches had been slipped.

Until 1927, the 'Counties' were the heaviest engines allowed on the Bristol-Birmingham GW services via Honeybourne. Another run just before the First World War with Stafford Road's 1912 built *3829 County of Merioneth* and its regular driver, J. Moore, was very sprightly, covering the twenty-five miles between Stratford-on-Avon and Birmingham Snow Hill in 30 minutes 10 seconds (28 minutes net) but the load was only a minuscule 85 tons. It sustained 57mph up the long 7½ mile 1 in 150 to Wood End and touched 72 at Yardley Wood before a p-way slack at Tyseley. 3810 *County Kildare* had a much heavier load, 304 tons and took 33 minutes 36 seconds (32 minutes net allowing for signal checks approaching Birmingham) – a slower start, up the mile 1 in 75 climb to Wilmcote (25½mph) with an excellent 49mph minimum at Wood End and 70 at Yardley Wood.

3829 was again in action on the Birmingham-Paddington two hour services introduced

Leamington – Paddington

3829 *County of Merioneth*
200/210 tons

Distance Miles	Location	Times mins secs	Speed mph
0.0	Leamington	00.00	
6.1	Southam Road	08.41	
11.1	Fenny Compton	13.26	63.2 ave
16.2	Cropredy	17.56	68.0 ave
19.8	Banbury	20.49	74.4 ave
24.9	Aynho Junction	24.51	76.5 ave
30.1	Ardley	29.55	50½ min
33.9	Bicester	33.10	
43.2	Ashendon Jcn	41.16	69.5 ave /75 max (est)
47.2	Haddenham	45.30	
52.6	Princes Risborough	50.36	
55.1	Saunderton Summit	53.14	50½ min
60.8	High Wycombe	59.10	57.0 ave
65.6	Beaconsfield	64.12	57.6 ave
69.9	Gerrards Cross	67.56	68.8 ave
77.0	Northolt Jcn	73.43	77½ max
82.7	Park Royal	78.29	sigs
87.3	Paddington	88.33	(85 ½ net)

3829 seems to have been a particularly good engine – or it was the skill of its regular driver that brought it much into prominence in recorded runs of the period? Cecil J Allen spent a day on London-Birmingham two-hour trains after the new Bicester route earthworks had consolidated and trains had been accelerated. The two down runs were with 'Saint' 4-6-0s, and the first up run with 4-4-2 *La France*, but the last up run on the 4.50pm Birmingham allowed just two

after the Bicester route opening and I show below an outline of its excellent run.

hours with stops at Leamington and Banbury again sported 3829 *County of Merioneth*, although with only 130 tons. This run was notable for its high speeds. It had done so well that it had to wait time at Banbury, then shot away and descended from Ardley down to Brill at a steady 80-82mph. This was nothing compared to the last sprint, however, for the (allegedly rough-riding) 3829 touched 86½mph through Denham, matching exactly the maximum speed of the smooth running De Glehn atlantic earlier in the day. Checks after Royal Oak meant that the train was five minutes late in, the net time being 69 minutes for the 67.5 miles. Further non-stop Leamington-Paddington runs were recorded on the new expresses with both 'Flowers' and 'Counties', the former achieving net times of 86-90 minutes with 120-135 tons, whilst three 'Counties' took 86-91 net minutes with 180-215 tons. The best run of a batch of four 'Counties' was again with 3829 which got its 215 ton load through Banbury in a very sharp 20 minutes 50 seconds (almost identical to the log above) and continued well, passing Aynho Junction at 76½mph although easing thereafter, without achieving any further high speeds.

3829 *County* of *Merioneth* at Ruislip on an up Birmingham-Paddington express. This locomotive featured strongly in the best runs of the Birmingham two-hour trains immediately before the First World War, c1913.
(J.M.Bentley Collection/Real Photographs)

3822 *County* of *Brecon* and another 'County' 4-4-0 which have double-headed a heavy North & West express from the West of England to Manchester from Bristol, at Shrewsbury, uncoupled and ready to be replaced by a LNWR engine, c1912.
(GW Trust)

In 1917 some of the best running – as in the Second World War – was over the North & West route and there are two logs with 1904 built 'Counties' and heavy loads which the 4-4-0s managed very competently. Of six runs quoted by O.S. Nock in his 1954 book, *Fifty Years of Western Express Running,* the two 'County' runs were faster with equal or heavier loads than the runs with 4-6-0 'Saints', and were significantly better than the taper-boilered 'Badminton', 4116 with a lesser load.

Hereford – Shrewsbury, 1917

Distance Location		Times	Speeds	Sch	Times	Speeds	Sch
		3834 *County of Somerset*			3832 *County of Wilts*		
		330 tons			410 tons		
Miles		mins secs	mph		mins secs	mph	
0.0	Hereford	00.00		T	00.00		T
7.5	Dinmore	10.29			11.25		
12.6	Leominster	16.00	55.6 ave	T	16.43	54.6 ave	¾ L
18.9	Woofferton	22.44	56.0 ave	¾ E	23.00	60.5 ave	½ E
23.5	Ludlow	27.48		¼ E	27.05	69.0 ave	1 E
28.1	Onibury	33.22	50.2 ave		-		
31.1	Craven Arms	36.56	51.4 ave	T	36.26	49.0 ave	½ E
35.6	Marshbrook	42.28	49.0 ave		-		
38.2	Church Stretton	46.00	44.2 ave	1 E	47.18	34 min	¼ L
44.6	Dorrington	51.58	64.0 ave		53.10	69 max	
51.0	Shrewsbury	61.37		2½ E	63.30 (62 net)		½ E

An unidentified 'County' runs into Newport with a Manchester-Cardiff train in the early 1920s.
(J. Hodge Collection)

3834 went out hard from Hereford, but eased after Dinmore until opened up for the five mile 1 in 103/112 climb to Church Stretton, the fastest climb of any of the six runs compared by Nock. The run with 3832 with the 410ton load was superb with speed reaching the low 70s around Woofferton and a very respectable climb to Church Stretton, beating the 64 minute overall schedule geared for a train half this weight. In the southbound direction, Nock records six runs of which only one was a 4-4-0 'County', the rest being 4-6-0 'Saints'. 3825 *County of Denbigh* with 300 tons beat the 65 minute schedule by just ¼ minute, dropping three minutes from Shrewsbury to Church Stretton, surmounting the 1 in 100 at 28mph, but racing down the bank through Craven Arms at 76½ mph, averaging 65mph from Craven Arms to Ludlow, 66mph on to Woofferton and a steady 60mph thereafter.

At the amalgamation of the 'Big Four' in 1923, the forty 'Counties' were spread over the system, as follows:

Bristol Bath Road:	7
Wolverhampton:	6
Swindon:	6
Worcester:	4
Shrewsbury:	4
Pontypool:	3
Westbury:	3
Reading:	2 (one normally as standby engine to cover failures on the mainline)
Hereford:	1
Landore:	1
Banbury:	1
Taunton:	1
Old Oak Common	1 (also as standby at Ranelagh Bridge?)

3812 *County* of Cardigan runs into Shrewsbury with a Chester-Wolverhampton-London train whilst a double-headed LNWR pair (train engine a 'George V' 4-4-0) approaches from Crewe with a Manchester-Bristol train, c1920. The LNWR engines will change here for a GW 4-4-0 or 29XX 4-6-0.
(J.M. Bentley Collection)

3815 *County* of Hants with a Hereford-Shrewsbury stopping train formed with LNWR/LMS coaching stock, on the water troughs between Ludlow and Bromford, early 1920s.
(GW Trust)

3829 *County of Merioneth* at Aldermaston with a Paddington-Weymouth express, March 1921. (GW Trust)

3814 *County* of Chester on a Birmingham express c1920. (J.M. Bentley Collection)

3803 *County* Cork pilots a 29XX 'Saint' on a heavy up express, c1923. (GW Trust)

3803 *County* Cork with a down semi-fast train at Langley, c1923. (GW Trust)

3804 *County* Dublin leaving Paddington with a down express, c1923. (GW Trust)

3804 *County* *Dublin,* equipped with the bogie 8-wheel tender off *The Great Bear,* on the up main line between Sonning and Twyford with a semi-fast train from Oxford, c1926. (GW Trust)

3809 *County* *Wexford* on a Wolverhampton Paddington express, c 1923. (GW Trust)

3812 *County* of Cardigan stands at Cardiff General ready to depart with a Cardiff-Paddington service, c1923.
(GW Trust)

3811 *County* of Bucks departs Paddington with a semi-fast service for Oxford, c1925.
(GW Trust)

3813 *County of Carmarthen* at West Drayton on an up express, c1925.
(J.M. Bentley Collection/ Photomatic)

3813 *County of Carmarthen* on a down express at Scours Lane west of Reading, c1925.
(J.M. Bentley Collection)

3813 *County* of *Carmarthen* departs Paddington with a down Oxford semi-fast, passing a new 57XX pannier tank, c1929. (GW Trust)

3821 *County* of *Bedford* on a long freight at Hayes, c1927. (GW Trust)

3822 *County* of *Brecon* at an unidentified location, c1925. (GW Trust)

3829 *County* of *Merioneth* at Paddington backing out to Ranelagh Bridge after arriving with an express, 13 May 1922. (GW Trust)

3836 *County* of Warwick (ex 3479) departs Paddington with a down express, 1927.
(GW Trust)

3803 *County* Cork at Reading on a two-coach stopping train from Didcot, c1923. From the condition of the engine, it is probable that this was a running in turn from Swindon, after a Works overhaul.
(J.M. Bentley Collection)

After the war, the two-hour Paddington-Birmingham schedules were restored, but the trains were hauled primarily by 4-6-0 locomotives. The 2.55pm Birmingham was allowed two stops – at Leamington and Banbury – within the schedule, a return diagram for the Old Oak 'Star' off the 9.10am Paddington. On one occasion, the 4-6-0 was failed on arrival at Wolverhampton and 4-4-0 3821 *County of Bedford* was provided as substitute power with 315 tons gross. It performed excellently, virtually holding time, and covering the last 67.5 miles from Banbury in a net time of 70 minutes – the schedule:

Birmingham Snow Hill-Paddington c 1921

2.55pm Birmingham-Paddington
3821 County of Bedford
294/315 tons

Distance/Location Miles		Times Mins secs	Speed mph	Schedule
0.0	Birmingham Snow Hill	00.00	T	
3.2	Tyseley	05.20		
10.4	Knowle	12.35	67	
12.9	Lapworth	14.35	76½	
17.1	Hatton	18.15	60*	¼ L
21.3	Warwick	21.35	79	
23.3	Leamington	23.55		2 E
		00.00	T	
6.1	Southam Road	10.20	45½	
11.1	Fenny Compton	17.10	sigs	
16.2	Cropredy	23.10	67	
19.8	Banbury	27.10	(25 net)	3 L
		00.00		5 L
5.1	Aynho Junction	07.55	60	
10.3	Ardley	13.25	50	
14.1	Bicester	16.45	82½	
20.1	Brill	21.15	62 ½	
23.3	Ashendon Junction	24.25	60*	4½ L
27.4	Haddenham	28.20	62 ½	
32.8	Princes Risborough	33.55	53	4 L
36.0	Saunderton	37.45	46½	
41.0	High Wycombe	43.10	71½/35*	4 L
45.8	Beaconsfield	48.55	56½/52½	
52.7	Denham	55.05	79	
57.2	Northolt Junction	58.45	72½	3¾ L
59.7	Greenford	60.45	76½	3¾ L
62.9	Park Royal	63.20		
64.2	Old Oak West Junction	65.35	sigs*	3½ L
	Subway Junction	-	sigs*	
67.5	Paddington	73.45	(70 net)	6¾ L

In their final years before withdrawal in 1930-33, they were relegated to stopping and semi-fast services between London and Oxford via both Reading and High Wycombe/Princes Risborough; Wolverhampton and Chester/Leamington & Banbury; Swindon-Bristol-Taunton; and Hereford-Shrewsbury. However, right at the last moment, after 'Halls' had taken over most of the Bristol-Birmingham services via Stratford-on-Avon, one of the surviving 'Counties' featured in an excellent run. 3812 *County of Cardigan*, the only one of the 1906 batch to exceed a million miles, had a 246/255 load and completed the twenty-five miles from Stratford to Birmingham in 29 minutes 55 seconds (28½ minutes net) after stalling leaving Stratford unusually without a banker out of the platform. It then cleared the 1 in 75 to Wilmcote at 31mph, hurried up to 68 mph in the dip after the climb, ascended the seven miles of 1 in 150/181 to Wood End and Earlswood Lakes at 54/55½ mph respectively and then dashed away to 73mph at Halls Green before signal checks causing a loss of a minute and a half delayed the entry to Birmingham Snow Hill.

Their final allocation was:

Swindon:	9
Oxford:	8
Reading:	5
Leamington:	4
Tyseley:	3
Weston-super-Mare:	3
Didcot:	2
Hereford:	2
Westbury:	1
Bristol Bath Road:	1
Pontypool:	1
Old Oak Common	1

3806 *County* Kildare at Bentley Heath with a ten coach Birmingham-Paddington express, c1923.
(J.M. Bentley Collection)

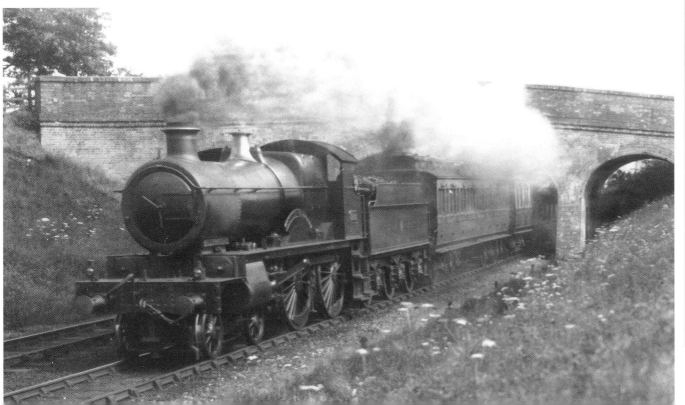

3809 *County* Wexford with a Birmingham express, north of Oxford c1923.
(J.M. Bentley Collection)

3810 *County* *Wicklow* at Knowle & Dorridge with a London-Birmingham express, c1923.
(GW Trust)

3814 *County* *of Chester* at Bentley Heath with a Paddington-Birmingham express, c1923.
(J.M. Bentley Collection/L W Good)

3814 *County* of Chester leaving Harbury Tunnel with a Birmingham-Paddington express, c1923.
(GW Trust)

3819 *County* of Salop with an Oxford-Wolverhampton train on Lapworth troughs, c1923.
(MLS/Bob Miller Collection/G. Tidey)

3819 *County* of Salop with a lightweight Birmingham-Paddington express on Lapworth troughs, c1923.
(GW Trust)

3837 *County* of Stafford (ex 3480) at Knowle & Dorridge with a mixed parcels and milk train, c1923.
(GW Trust)

It will be noted that sixteen were on local, semi-fast and parcels services in the London Division, with Old Oak Common hanging on to its one engine (although not the same one), with seven in the Birmingham area and fourteen around Swindon and Bristol. In their last couple of years, they replaced double-framed 4-4-0s on local trains in these areas. They were finally made redundant by the arrival of the 'Halls' from 1929. The 1904 built 3833 (ex 3476) was the first to be withdrawn in February 1930 and surprisingly the 1904 3834 (ex 3477) was the last survivor, condemned in November 1933. Four 'Counties' topped a million miles in traffic, including three of the 1904 build (3832, 3834 and 3836) and just one of the 1906 build (3812). The 1904 batch mileages ranged from 900,000 to a million, the 1906 twenty engines averaged around 800-900,000 and the final 1911-12 build between 700,000 and 800,000 with 3821 condemned in September 1931 the lowest of the class at just over 690,000.

3808 *County* Limerick passing Iver with a Weymouth-Paddington express, 5 August 1929. (GW Trust)

3814 *County* of Chester at Southampton Terminus after working a Cardiff-Southampton train, c1927. (GW Trust)

3815 *County of Hants* still working a Paddington-Birmingham express past Bentley Heath as late as 1929.
(J.M. Bentley Collection)

3816 *County of Leicester* on a Torquay-Wolverhampton train passing Cheltenham (Racecourse), 21 July 1924.
(GW Trust)

3823 *County* of *Carnarvon* at Reading on the 12.30pm Paddington-Weymouth, 13 March 1926.
(MLS/Bob Miller Collection/K. Nunn)

3834 *County* of *Somerset* (ex 3477) leaving Salisbury on a Dover-Bristol train formed with ex SE&CR and Southern Railway stock, c1927.
(GW Trust)

An unidentified 'County' with a train of empty milk siphons passing Sonning, c1925.
(MLS/Bob Miller Collection)

The 'Counties' seem to have developed a poor reputation, eclipsed by Churchward's 4-6-0s and not as high profile as famous 4-4-0 contemporaries on other railways. They were undoubtedly rough-riding engines, especially when due for heavy overhaul, but the evidence is that they performed well on the road and drivers were prepared to run them fast despite their rough-riding propensity. They – along with the GW's other 4-4-0s – were withdrawn after only 20-30 years' life, because the Depression of the late 20s and early 30s and consequent reduction in traffic and need for economies coincided with the increase in standard 4-6-0s, in particular the 1929 'Halls', which took over the mixed traffic and cross-country work on which the 4-4-0s had finished their days.

3818 *County of Radnor* moves off to Ranelagh Bridge after arriving at Paddington, 6 June 1931. A 22XX 'County Tank' stands alongside.
(GW Trust)

3818 *County* of Radnor at Kensal Green with a Paddington-Reading-Oxford semi-fast train, August 1931. Despite looking in reasonable condition, 3818 was withdrawn at the end of the month.
(J.M. Bentley Collection/ Photomatic)

3814 *County* of Chester on the Kensington milk empties passing Acton Yard, c1927.
(GW Trust)

3815 *County of Hants* on a lightweight parcels train, including siphons for milk churn traffic, near Newbury, c1929. (GW Trust)

3833 *County of Dorset* (ex 3476) was the first 'County' to be withdrawn in February 1930. It is seen here a few years earlier on a parcels train at an unidentified location. (GW Trust)

3835 *County* of Devon (formerly 3478) with a London-bound fish, parcels and empty stock train at Fenny Compton, just before its withdrawal in January 1931. (GW Trust)

Hornby has produced a model of a 4-4-0 'County', 3821 *County of Bedford* and has now reproduced it in their Railroad' series as 3835 *County of Devon.* Unfortunately, the latter is historically incorrect as 3835 was originally 3478 built in 1904 (and renumbered in 1912) with stepped running plate over the cylinders and straight continuation under the cab and not the later curved plate introduced for the 1911-12 batch, 3821-3830.

The Hornby 4-4-0 'County' model, 3821 *County of Bedford*, which is correctly shown with curved running plate from bufferbeam above the cylinders and below the cab. (David Maidment)

Chapter 2

THE COUNTY 4-4-2 TANK ENGINES

Design & Construction

The first Churchward 4-4-2 tank engine was built at Swindon in 1905. Despite the success of the 2-6-2T, No.99 and its production successors, the 3100 class, the new Locomotive Superintendent included a 6ft 8½in 4-4-2T in his range of standard locomotives for the GW. Initially, the 3100 class were seen as freight and banking locomotives, and the new engine numbered 2221 was conceived as its passenger equivalent, the tank engine version of the outside cylinder 4-4-0 'County' class, the first ten of which had been constructed the previous year. Inevitably these new engines became known as the 'County Tanks'. At the time, the suburban trains from Paddington to Reading, Newbury and Oxford were the preserve of the 2-4-0 'Metro Tanks' and the ungainly 2-4-2T '3600 class'. With their large diameter coupled wheels – very unusual for a tank engine – they were clearly intended for the longer-distance semi-fast suburban trains. This is clear from their provision with water pick-up apparatus (two-way as they were expected to work bunker-first) although these were removed in the 1920s. As the 31XX

One of the first batch of ten built in 1905-6, 2226 in operation shortly after delivery, 1906
(MLS/Bob Miller Collection/ Pouteau postcard)

engines with similar standard parts had already been comprehensively and successfully tested, there was no prolonged testing of 2221 before the production batch was constructed.

As indicated, the main dimensions of the 'County Tank' were similar to the 'County' 4-4-0. As well as the 6ft 8½in coupled wheels, the bogie wheels were 3ft 2in. The trailing pony truck wheel diameter was 3ft 8in. The two outside cylinders were 18in x 30in stroke as for the 4-4-0. The tank engine was fitted with the smaller standard No.2 boiler, long-coned but short smoke-box, pressed at 195lbs psi, giving a tractive effort (at 85%) of 20,010 lbs. The grate area was 20.35sqft and total heating surface was 1,517.89sqft. Bunker capacity was three tons of coal and the tanks could hold 2,000 gallons of water. The prototype had cab flush with tanks and bunker (later engines had slightly wider tanks and bunker). The engine's axle-load was 19 tons and total weight, 75 tons.

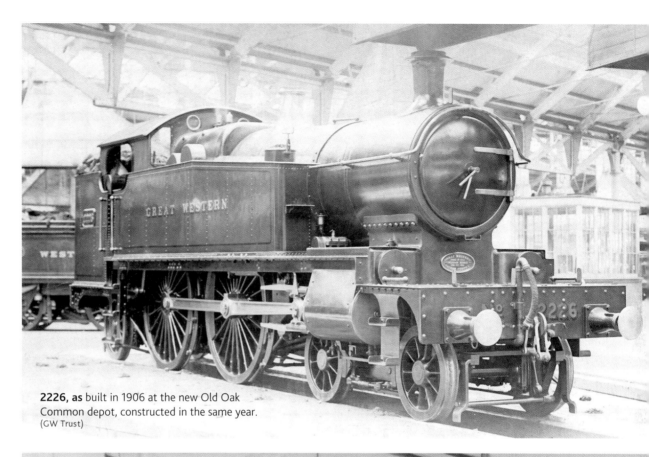

2226, as built in 1906 at the new Old Oak Common depot, constructed in the same year.
(GW Trust)

The class prototype, 2221, superheated, with topfeed, narrow cast-iron chimney, extended bunker and numberplate in the standard position on the bunker rather than on the tank sides as this engine only had after construction. It is unique in having cab sides flush with side tanks and bunker. The locomotive is seen waiting its next turn at Paddington, c1923.
(GW Trust)

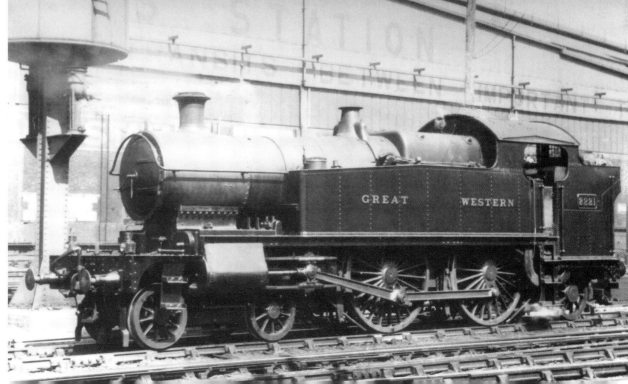

2221, at the end of its career, c1930. (MLS Collection)

One of the initial batch, 2230, was equipped with the heavier No.4 boiler similar to the 4-4-0s, but this increased the weight by around 3½ tons and would have increased the axle-load, and the experiment was short-lived, it being exchanged for a No.2 boiler in January 1907 having run less than 7,000 miles with the larger boiler. There was a proposal to build a 4-4-4T with a No.4 boiler and this may have been a trial, but the latter design was never progressed – however, a drawing exists (see appendix).

The initial production batch (2222-2230) had number plates on their bunkers, and the words 'Great Western' on the tank side without the GW crest. (2221 had its numberplate on the tank sides.) They had cast-iron chimneys and 2221 had steam sanding gear although this was removed in 1906. A second batch (2231-2240) was built in 1908-9, which differed by being fitted with copper-cap chimneys and larger vacuum cylinders. Some of the earlier engines had received copper-cap chimneys by this time and all were

now receiving the livery including the GW crest. 2225 suddenly appeared in a chocolate lake livery like some of the GW coaches at this time, and was transferred to the Bristol/Swindon area for further trials.

Superheating for these locomotives, as for many of GW's locomotive fleet, commenced in 1910 and was completed by 1914. A final batch, 2241-2250, was built in 1912, already superheated. These had curved front footplating, topfeed and extended smoke-boxes. The superheated engines had a

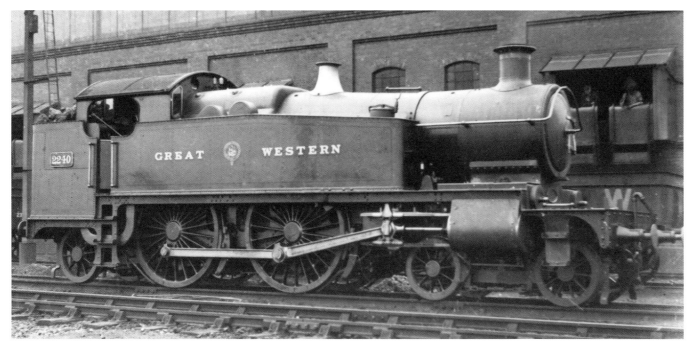

2240, the last of the second batch of 'County Tanks', built in 1908-9, at Old Oak Common, c1910.
(GW Trust)

reduced total heating surface of 1,316.14sqft, although other detailed differences between the last ten and the first twenty locomotives remained. Boiler pressure was standardised at 200lbs psi from 1919 increasing the tractive effort to 20,530lbs and bunker tops were extended backwards between 1922 and 1925, some getting recessed fenders at the rear to hold the upper lamp iron. Because these engines ran over the London area mainlines, some received ATC apparatus early in 1908 and most others around 1915-16. Most engines in the last years before withdrawal got cast-iron chimneys again.

2241, first of the 1911-12 'lot' of the 4-4-2Ts, in photographic works grey.
(GW Trust)

2243, of the final batch of 'County Tanks' built in 1912, at Old Oak Common, c1912.
(GW Trust)

New 2241 at Old Oak Common with an unidentified 'Star', c1912.
(GW Trust)

2234 inside Old Oak Common depot, c1912.
(MLS Collection/G. Tidey)

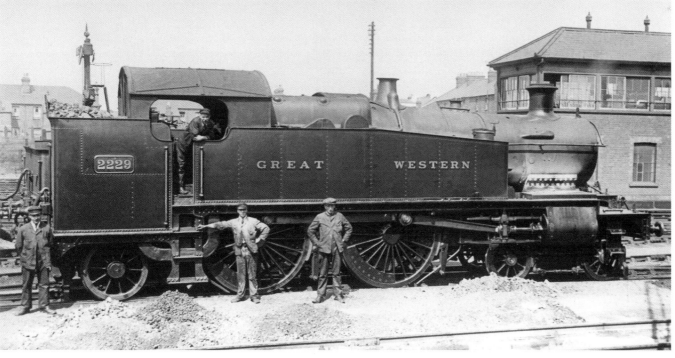

2229 posing at Slough with its proud crew, August 1920.
(GW Trust)

2234 built in October 1908 with copper capped chimney painted over, tall safety valve cover and topfeed, but still with straight-backed bunker, at Old Oak Common, c1920.
(GW Trust)

2239 built in January 1909, with copper cap chimney painted over after the First World War, tall safety valve cover with topfeed and extended bunker, at Didcot shed, c1923.
(GW Trust)

2247, built superheated in July 1912, at Old Oak Common, with topfeed and straight backed bunker, c1920.
(MLS Collection)

2222 of the initial batch, with narrow cast-iron chimney and extended bunker, at Westbourne Park, c1925.
(GW Trust)

2223 with large copper cap chimney and straight-backed bunker, on Slough shed, c1923.
(GW Trust)

2243 with painted over copper cap chimney and extended bunker, at Old Oak Common, in front of a 'Castle', c1925.
(GW Trust)

Rear view of 2247 with extended bunker, opposite Ranelagh Bridge outside Paddington station, c1925.
(GW Trust)

2229 waiting attention outside Old Oak Common 'Factory', c1930.
(GW Trust)

The construction of the 61XX 2-6-2Ts with 225lbs psi boilers in 1931 by Charles Collett for the London suburban services marked the end of the 2221 class and sixteen of the class had been withdrawn by October 1932. The last in service were 2235, 2242 and 2246 at Reading, condemned in January, September and November 1935 respectively. 2243, withdrawn in December 1934, was retained at Old Oak Common to perform carriage heating duties and was not sent to Swindon for scrapping until August 1939. Locomotive ages ranged from twenty to thirty years and total mileage between 583,000 and 876,000, and they were withdrawn because of the appearance of more suitable locomotives for the work, rather than life-expiry. The size of wheels made them capable of fast running but their lack of adhesion and large wheels made them less suitable for frequently stopping services and the heavier trains as commuting into London increased.

2226 in store at Old Oak Common, c1933.
(MLS /A.C Gilbert Collection/ G. Tidey)

2232 after an 'Intermediate' repair at Swindon (note: just smokebox repainted), 26 April 1931. To the rear is 'Metro Tank' 1407.
(GW Trust)

One of the last survivors – from the earliest batch – 2225 at Oxford shed with a 'Star' 4-6-0, 21 April 1934 (GW Trust)

The prototype 4-4-2T, 2221, at the Swindon Dump awaiting breaking up, 1933. Note that, alone of its class, it has retained cab sides flush with bunker and tanks. 2244 is stored behind it. (GW Trust)

2246 withdrawn from service after sustaining collision damage, here at the Swindon Dump, c1936. 2246 was the last 'County Tank' in active service, being withdrawn from Reading depot in November 1935.
(GW Trust)

2243 at Old Oak Common – the last survivor of the class, retained for several years after the demise of the rest for heating of empty carriages before entering service – seen here after eventual withdrawal, 7 May 1939.
(MLS Collection)

Operation

Apart from 2221, which spent its first six months being tested in the Bristol-Swindon area, the initial batch all went to the London motive power division to cover the faster suburban services to Reading, Newbury and Oxford, and the High Wycombe-Princes Risborough/Oxford/Aylesbury route. In 1906, 2222-2230 were all working from the brand new Old Oak Common depot, although 2225 moved to Reading for three months in 1907, whilst two of the original batch were transferred to Slough in 1909, and a further one in 1910. The 1908-9 batch were spread between Old Oak Common, Slough and Reading, with the majority at the London depot. Nine of the new 1912 built batch went to Old Oak Common in 1912, with some of the older engines moving to Slough and Reading. By 1912, Old Oak had fourteen on its books, increasing to seventeen in 1913 and maintained a fleet between twelve and fifteen engines until 1920, when the average allocation there fell to ten-twelve, with four going to the Wolverhampton division.

In 1902, slip working was introduced on some London suburban services with coaches for Windsor being slipped at Slough from services bound for Henley or Oxford. The joint line with the Great Central to Denham, Gerrards Cross and High Wycombe was open for suburban services from 2 April 1906, and the new 'County Tanks' allocated to Old Oak Common would have found immediate employment on these

2224 at Royal Oak backing towards Paddington station, 1909. (GW Trust)

2223 with an up stopping train leaving Twyford after being superheated, c1911.
(GW Trust)

2225 at Slough with a semi-fast train for Reading and Oxford, c1907.
(GW Trust)

as well as the faster services to Henley and Reading. There were five new services each way from Paddington to Aylesbury and five to Oxford via Princes Risborough and Thame. After the Birmingham route via Bicester was opened in 1910, a morning and evening service to Banbury was implemented with either 'County' or 'County Tank' haulage, allowed just 30 or 31 minutes for the 26.4 miles from Paddington, mainly against the grade and faster than the 9.10am express two-hour Birmingham train which was allowed 32 minutes. The morning commuter services from Gerrards Cross were allowed 28 minutes for the 17.5 miles to Paddington, 23 minutes from Denham (15 miles), 18 from Ruislip (11.8 miles), and 13 minutes from Greenford (7.8 miles) involving some sharp start-to-stop times on these falling gradients before slowing for Old Oak Common and the approach to Paddington station. The evening services – against the gradient – were also tightly timed, with a 12 minute allowance to Greenford, 20 to Ruislip, 24 to Denham, 30 to Gerrards Cross and 38 minutes to Beaconsfield (21.5 miles). By 1913, when these services would have been monopolised by the 'County Tanks', there were five trains each way between Paddington and Henley, slipping coaches at Slough for the Windsor branch plus two evening services for Oxford which slipped coaches at Slough for Taplow, and Maidenhead for High Wycombe. In the book *Great Western London Suburban Services* by Thomas B Peacock (reprinted by the Oakwood Press in 1970) the author states '(that) the 'County Tanks' were responsible for outstanding performance on fast heavy trains between Paddington and Windsor, Henley and Reading.'

A '**County** Tank' of the first 1905/6 series between Old Oak Common and Acton with a down semi-fast train, passing an outside framed Armstrong 0-6-0, c1906.
(MLS Collection/Locomotive Publishing Company)

2236 of the 1908-9 series at Paddington, c1910.
(GW Trust)

2248 of the 1912 series on the 6.20pm Paddington-Windsor near Dawley, 4 June 1914. The first coach is a broad gauge 'convertible'.
(J. Hodge Collection)

2234 shunting at Aylesbury, 24 June1916.
(J. Hodge Collection)

2242 at speed on Goring troughs with a train that purports to be the 9am Bristol-Paddington, 14.3.1915. A tank engine on a long distance train is a rarity and one wonders whether it had replaced a failure at Swindon or Didcot or whether the GW were short of power for such passenger trains in the middle of the First World War (or whether the photographer had mistaken the train's identity!).
(J. Hodge Collection)

2233 at Paddington alongside GW pacific *The Great Bear*. The 'County Tank' is probably on the 6.20pm Paddington-Windsor, and 111 on the 6.30pm to Bristol, its regular diagram, c1910. (GW Trust)

2244 coaling at Old Oak Common depot, c1920. (GW Trust)

A 'County Tank' performs ECS duties, entering Paddington station with the stock of a down express, 4 August 1920. The first vehicle is a rare Churchward 70ft 'Dreadnought' Brake. (GW Trust)

2225 taking water at Paddington between turns, c1920. (GW Trust)

Over the years a few examples were tried in different locations, although the London area always remained their main sphere of operation until their replacement by the 61XX class. Other locations at which they worked, mainly for short periods, were:

Trowbridge/Westbury: 2221 (1906 – 1918), 2228, 2237 for short periods (working locals to Westbury/Bristol/Hungerford/Reading)

Swindon: 2221 (1919), 2222, 2229, 2230 (short periods in 1907-8 and 1915)

Newton Abbot: 2226, 2236 (very short periods in 1907 and 1911)

Newport: 2230 (1907-08), 2250 (two months in 1918)

Landore: 2224 (two months in 1911)

Wolverhampton: 2223/25/26/30/42/43/46 (for 18 months in 1920-21, replaced by 31XX)

Chester: 2246 (two months in 1920)

Taunton: 2224 (four months in 1921)

Most of these trials appear to have been unsuccessful, the work being

more suitable for the increasing number of 5ft 8in wheeled 2-6-2Ts. To give a snapshot, the allocation at the amalgamation of the 'Big Four' at the end of 1922 was as follows:

2221	Slough
2222	Slough
2223	Slough
2224	Slough
2225	Aylesbury
2226	Slough
2227	Old Oak Common
2228	Slough
2229	Slough
2230	Aylesbury
2231	Reading
2232	Slough
2233	Old Oak Common
2234	Slough
2235	Aylesbury
2236	Reading
2237	Slough
2238	Old Oak Common
2239	Aylesbury
2240	Reading
2241	Old Oak Common
2242	Slough
2243	Slough
2244	Reading
2245	Old Oak Common
2246	Slough
2247	Old Oak Common
2248	Slough
2249	Slough
2250	Slough

Many of the faster suburban services, including the slip-coach working, were suspended in the First World War between 1917 and 1919 and the few remaining slip coaches still running on suburban trains in 1939 were suspended at the start of the Second World War and never restored. The 'County Tanks' resumed their fast train working, especially after 1922,

2227 approaching Paddington with an up stopping passenger train, c1925.
(GW Trust)

with the 4.40pm Paddington-Banbury accelerated by a couple of minutes to Denham, Gerrards Cross and Beaconsfield, although in the late 1920s double-framed 4-4-0s and the 'County' 38XX would take over the Oxford via Princes Risborough and the Banbury train. Half the class was based at Slough by this time and none of the 'County Tanks' were then outside the London division. At the end Didcot received three in 1933/4 and Oxford just one (2225) in 1934, but by this time most of the Old Oak and Slough engines had been replaced by the Collett 61XX 'Prairie Tanks' and had been withdrawn. The last three (2235, 2242 and 2246) were withdrawn from Reading depot during 1935.

Despite searching for logs of performance of the 'County Tanks', I can trace no records either in the 'Locomotive Practice and Performance ' articles of the *Railway Magazine* or in the archives of the Railway Performance Society. They appear to have been used mainly on the semi-fast services in the London area, with the all-stations stopping trains remaining by and large the duty of 'Metro' 2-4-0Ts, the 36XX 2-4-2Ts, and the 39XX 2-6-2Ts (the rebuilt 'Dean Goods' some of which transferred to the London area in the late 1920s) until the 1931 built 61XX replaced all of them. With their large driving wheels and moderate adhesion, they would have struggled to accelerate heavy stopping trains, as I discovered in 1958 when I travelled on an eight-coach suburban train (the 6.20pm Paddington-Reading) behind the 6ft 8in 4-4-0, *City of Truro*. However, once on the move they would – like their tender 4-4-0 counterparts – have displayed a good turn of speed and I'm sure speeds in the 65-75mph range between Paddington and Reading, between Reading and Didcot, or especially between Beaconsfield and Ruislip, would have been commonplace, even if the riding was a bit rough, as apparently they shared that reputation with the 38XX 'Counties'.

2232 at Portobello Junction waiting its next turn, 10 April 1928.
(J. Hodge Collection)

2236 departing
Paddington bunker first
on a suburban train to
Reading, c1923.
(GW Trust)

2224 with a local service
at an unknown location,
thought to be on the
'Berks & Hants' west of
Reading or further west
during its short stay at
Taunton depot in 1921.
(GW Trust)

2223 departing from Paddington with a down stopping service, April 1927.
(GW Trust)

2234 passing West Drayton with an Oxford-Paddington semi-fast service, c1925.
(GW Trust)

2242 leaving Paddington station with a down stopping suburban service, c1923. The first vehicle is a Dean 'convertible' coach. (GW Trust)

2240 at Hayes with a Paddington – Oxford semi-fast train, c1925. (MLS Collection/Photomatic)

The prototype 2221 on an up stopping service approaching Ealing Broadway, c1925.
(GW Trust)

2231 leaves Paddington with a ten-coach suburban set on a stopping service to Reading, c1928
(GW Trust)

2232 going off shed at Old Oak Common, c1928.
(GW Trust)

2235 on the down relief line at Sonning with a 3-coach suburban train to Reading, c1927.
(GW Trust)

One of the 1912 built 'County Tanks' at Twyford with a down stopping service, c1929.
(GW Trust)

2243 approaching Ealing Broadway with a semi-fast train for Oxford, c1929.
(GW Trust)

2235 at Paddington platform 9 with an empty stock train for Old Oak Common, 1932.
(MLS/G Coltas)

2244 at West Drayton with an up Windsor train, 6 June 1931.
(GW Trust)

The last member of the class, 2250, on a down semi-fast train at Kensal Green, c1931.
(GW Trust)

4600 Design, Construction & Operation

A smaller wheeled 4-4-2T was constructed at Swindon in November 1913. It was a version of the 2-6-2 smaller passenger tank engine (the 45XX class) and was numbered 4600. There were still a few 'metro 2-4-0' tanks being used on branch line work at this time and their replacement by the 4-4-2T was considered, though the success of the 45XX, the start of the First World War and increasing road competition for branch traffic meant that no further locomotives of this type were required. There was also a need for engines to work growing suburban traffic round Bristol and Birmingham – as distances between stations were shorter than London, it is assumed that smaller wheels were considered appropriate. However, the success of the 31XX 2-6-2Ts covered this area of developing work.

Its dimensions were 5ft 8in coupled wheels (larger than the 45XX and intended therefore to increase maximum speeds), with bogie wheels of 3ft 2in diameter, and trailing wheels of similar size. Its boiler was pressed at 200lbs psi, with grate area of just 16.6sqft and total heating surface of 1,271.86sqft. Two cylinders of 17in x 24in stroke were provided and the weight was 60 tons 12 cwt, significantly lighter than the 'County Tank', with just 16 ton axle-load. Tractive effort (at 85%) was 17,340lbs. The tank capacity was only 1,100 gallons indicating that short distance suburban or branch line work was anticipated.

It had curved footplating at front and rear, front end strengthening struts from the boiler saddle to buffer beam, copper-cap chimney and numberplates on the bunker side. The engine was superheated in 1918, reducing the total heating surface to 1,215.52sqft and reducing the total weight by 5 cwt.

It was initially allocated to Tyseley for suburban work in the Birmingham area. However, after the First World War and with the 31XX and 39XX 2-6-2Ts and 36XX 2-4-2Ts dominating the suburban trains both north and south of Birmingham, 4600 took up rural duties based at Neyland for the Pembroke Dock branch, where it remained until withdrawal in July 1925.

4600, the small-wheeled (5ft 8in) 4-4-2T, in Works grey, 1913. This was the only example built.
(MLS/Moore's postcard)

4600 at its first allocated shed, Tyseley, shortly after delivery, c1914.
(GW Trust)

4600, stored at Swindon a year before withdrawal, 24 May 1924.
(GW Trust)

Chapter 3

THE HAWKSWORTH COUNTY 4-6-0S

Design & Construction

Rumours of a new express locomotive began to swell around Swindon at the end of 1944. Some anticipated a pacific locomotive, others correctly a 4-6-0 with 6ft 3in driving wheels and a high pressure 280lbs psi boiler, a new departure for the GWR. Proposed initially as a development of the 'Modified Halls', and to be numbered 9900, the new engine appeared in August 1945 unnamed and numbered 1000. It was seen as the ultimate progression from the 1902 Churchward prototype two-cylinder 4-6-0, No.100. Like the Hawksworth 'Modified Hall', it had plate frames, including bogie, and initially 3-row superheater. The boiler was modelled on that of the LMS 8F, built at Swindon in the wartime era, and became known as the Swindon Standard No.15. Externally, the large experimental double-chimney was very noticeable, as was the new design of tender, flush-sided, 8ft 6in wide – 6in wider than the Collett 4,000 gallon tender – holding seven tons of coal and 4,000 gallons of water. Another departure from Swindon practice was the continuous splasher over all the coupled wheels. It is possible that the 4-6-0 was seen by Hawksworth as a test-bed for the pacific that had been conceived but not built because of wartime priorities.

The main dimensions of the new 4-6-0 were two outside 18½ in x 30in cylinders, 6ft 3in coupled wheels, 3ft diameter bogie wheels, with a total heating surface of 1,979sq. ft and grate area of 28.84sqft, with Stephenson link motion as for the other GW two-cylinder engines. It was fitted with a hopper ashpan for easier servicing at the end of its duty. Weight of the engine was 76 tons 17 cwt, with an axle-load of 19 tons 14 cwt, just inside the specification of 20 tons. The new design tender weighed 49 tons giving a total weight of 125 tons 17 cwt. Tractive effort was 32,580lbs and the route availability at first classified as E, and excluding work in South Wales, was later amended

The prototype Hawksworth 'County', No.1000 *County of Middlesex.*
(GWR official photo/MLS/Real Photographs)

Another official photograph of the prototype, 1000, seen from the side and before naming. 1000 was named *County of Middlesex* three months after construction in March 1946.
(GWR official photo/MLS Collection/Postcard)

to D 'red'. After 1000, the nineteen other locomotives of lot 354 built in 1945 and 1946 had standard GW copper-capped single chimneys. Because of the high boiler pressure, the class was theoretically the most powerful two-cylinder GW 4-6-0, on paper (taking tractive effort as the guideline) even more powerful than the four-cylinder 'Castles'.

After their initial nameless appearance, the engines were named as 'Counties', the first seven

The cab layout of a 'County' class 4-6-0, 1018 *County of Leicester*, photographed at Swindon during overhaul. (GW Trust)

being those counties through which the GWR ran from London to Cornwall. After that, starting from 1007, they were named in alphabetical order, thus:

1000	*County of Middlesex*	(named March 1946)
1001	*County of Bucks*	(named December 1947)
1002	*County of Berks*	(named May 1947)
1003	*County of Wilts*	(named August 1947)
1004	*County of Somerset*	(named August 1946)
1005	*County of Devon*	(named July 1946)
1006	*County of Cornwall*	(named April 1948)
1007	*County of Brecknock*	(named January 1948)
1008	*County of Cardigan*	(named June 1947)
1009	*County of Carmarthen*	(named February 1948)
1010	*County of Caernarvon*	(named December 1947)
1011	*County of Chester*	(named November 1947)
1012	*County of Denbigh*	(named July 1946)
1013	*County of Dorset*	(named January 1947)
1014	*County of Glamorgan*	(named March 1948)
1015	*County of Gloucester*	(named April 1947)
1016	*County of Hants*	(named September 1946)
1017	*County of Hereford*	(named March 1946)
1018	*County of Leicester*	(named April 1946)
1019	*County of Merioneth*	(named April 1946)

The last three were named before entering traffic, the rest on suitable occasions between March 1946 and April 1948, as indicated above. A further ten locomotives were constructed in 1946-47, ordered as lot 358 and were named before delivery to the traffic department. The name was mounted on the splasher on the left hand side, but was mounted separately in front of the reversing lever on the right. Some names that would otherwise have included the word 'shire' meaning 'county' were then abbreviated to avoid tautology – hence Bucks, Berks, Wilts, Chester, Hants, Salop rather than Berkshire, Wiltshire, Cheshire etc.:

1020 *County of Monmouth*
1021 *County of Montgomery*
1022 *County of Northampton*
1023 *County of Oxford*
1024 *County of Pembroke*
1025 *County of Radnor*
1026 *County of Salop*
1027 *County of Stafford*
1028 *County of Warwick*
1029 *County of Worcester*

Initial livery was GW green with the letters GW on the tender, and the London and Bristol coat of arms between. After nationalisation, they were painted in the BR mixed traffic livery of black with LNWR lining and red-backed name- and

1001 seen at the head of the *Torbay Express* at Newton Abbot in 1947, a year after construction and still unnamed. It was named *County of Bucks* in December 1947 after its first general overhaul. (GW Trust)

number-plates, and then in the mid-1950s they were treated to the full BR express livery of lined Brunswick green, which Swindon applied to a large number of GW designs in the late 1950s. A further thirty-five engines were planned making a total of sixty-five, but these were cancelled and 'Modified Halls' and a further batch of 3-row superheated 'Castles' were built instead, which indicates that the new engines were not seen as an immediate success. The 'Counties' delivered a heavy hammer-blow to the track, were accused by train crews of being rough-riding, and – like some other GW two-cylinder classes – exerted a strong fore-and-aft movement felt on the engine and in the first coaches behind the tender.

1026 *County of Salop* on Swindon shed, c1947. (GW Trust)

1010 *County of Caernarvon* at Reading at the head of an up express, 13.3.1948. Although three months after nationalisation the tender bears the GWR livery still, with the company's coat of arms between the G and W. (J.M Bentley Collection)

1002 *County of Berks* standing at the entrance to Bristol Bath Road shed opposite Temple Meads station, c1947. (GW Trust)

1017 *County* of Hereford being coaled in Wolverhampton Stafford Road shed, 7 August 1948. The tender has been repainted with the words 'British Railways' on the tender but still in GWR style. (GW Trust)

A year later, 1017 *County of Hereford* has been overhauled and repainted in the new BR mixed traffic lined black livery, but without any tender inscription as the BR lion and wheel totem had not yet been implemented. It is seen entering the large Old Oak Common roundhouse, past the block containing the shedmaster's and general offices, 3 July 1949. (J.M. Bentley Collection)

1026 *County* of *Salop* ex-works from Swindon heavy overhaul and repainted in the BR mixed traffic lined black with the new lion and wheel BR icon on the tender, 16 February 1950. (MLS Collection/W. Potter)

1007 *County* of *Brecknock* comes onto Bristol Bath Road depot after working a local service from Swindon, 4.9.1951. 1007 is now in the standard BR mixed traffic livery that was applied to all 'Counties' as they were classified 6MT and did not warrant the passenger green livery until Swindon Works began applying lined green to many classes after 1955. (MLS Collection/G. Harrop)

1008 *County* of *Cardigan* in BR mixed traffic lined black, c1954.
(J.M.Bentley Collection)

1022 *County* of *Northampton* paired with a Collett 4000 gallon tender at Swindon, February 1953. It is probable that 1022 was just parked next to this tender during an overhaul at Swindon Works and is unlikely to have been coupled to this tender in traffic.
(J.M. Bentley Collection/ Photomatic)

1012 *County* of *Denbigh* in BR mixed traffic lined black livery at Plymouth Laira depot, 12 July 1955. (R.C. Riley)

1004 *County* of *Somerset* at its home depot, Swindon, 30 January 1955. (GW Trust)

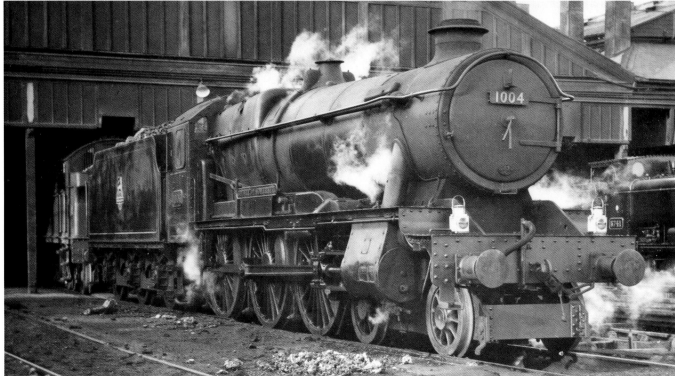

1021 *County of Montgomery* at Penzance, April 1955.
(J.M. Bentley Collection/ Photomatic)

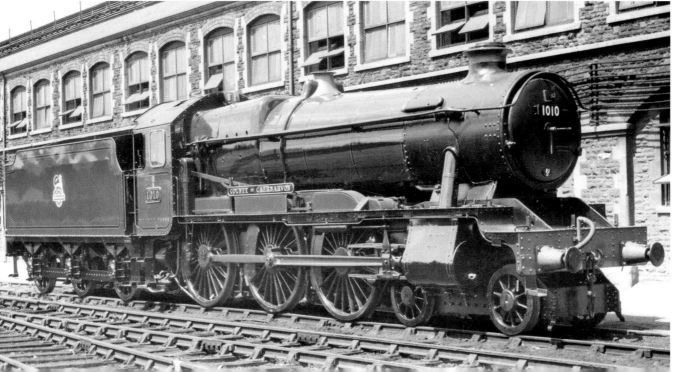

Laira's 1010 *County of Caernarvon* (note correct spelling compared with Churchward 4-4-0 3823) after overhaul and painting in BR lined green, 22 June 1955.
(GW Trust)

1018 *County* of *Leicester* at Swindon Works in typical pre-overhaul condition, its livery completed obscured by grime, c1955.
(MLS Collection)

Swindon's single chimney 1019 *County of Merioneth* alongside WD 2-8-0 90572 at Cardiff Canton shed, 22 September 1957.
(J. Hodge)

1021 *County of Montgomery* on the turntable at Canton depot, 3 May 1958. 1021 was one of the last 'Counties', with 1025 and 1029, to retain a single chimney.
(J. Hodge)

Shrewsbury's 1025
County of Radnor
at Cardiff Canton,
September 1958, also
still with single chimney.
(J. Hodge)

1029 *County* of
Worcester on Canton
shed, next to Hereford
based 5970 *Hengrave
Hall* and two double
chimney 9F 2-10-0s
in the background,
26 March 1959.
(J. Hodge)

Early experience indicated that these 4-6-0s suffered from indifferent steaming and lost time, particularly on the longer level stretches of GW main line where the 'Stars' and 'Castles' excelled. There were experiments with the draughting, culminating with the fitting of 1009 with a double stovepipe chimney in 1954, and its testing on the Swindon Plant 'rollers' and twenty-coach trains whilst working with the dynamometer car and indicator shelter. Its success led to the fitting of new double chimneys to all the 'Counties' including 1000, between May 1956 (1022) and October 1959 (1021). Whilst the double chimney was effective, it was aesthetically unsatisfactory, being very squat and lower than the safety valve bonnet. WR management considered improving this in 1961, but it was too near the demise of steam on the Western Region to be agreed and the idea was abandoned in August 1961. To economise on boiler repairs and as the high pressure was rarely utilised, the pressure was reduced to 250lbs from 1955 onwards, reducing their tractive effort to 29,090lbs. Most received four-row superheated boilers in the later years – these could be identified by a second casing on the smokebox under the handrail on the right hand side of the locomotive.

1009 *County of Carmarthen* fitted with a 'stovepipe' double chimney and under test with an indicator shelter and dynamometer car, 1954. This attempt to solve the steaming problem of the 'Counties' was relatively successful and led to the equipping of all the 'Counties' with a new design of double chimney from 1956 onwards.
(MLS Collection)

1009 *County* of *Carmarthen* with a new style double chimney built round the tested 'stovepipe' after a casual repair at Swindon Works, c1956. 1009 is still in BR lined black livery, the only 'County' to get the new double chimney whilst still in black livery.
(MLS Collection)

The third 'County' to be fitted with the new style 'squat' standard double chimney (in March 1957), Shrewsbury's 1016 *County of Hants*, at Old Oak Common, June 1957. 1016 retains a 3-row superheat boiler.
(J.M. Bentley Collection/Photomatic)

1000 *County* of *Middlesex* fitted with the new style double chimney after a full Works overhaul and repainting, March 1958 (GW Trust)

1002 *County* of Berks newly overhauled, fitted with a double chimney and repainted, at Swindon Works, 26 April 1959. Alongside also ex-works are 9F 92205 and a 'Modified Hall'. (R.C. Riley)

Neyland's 1001 *County of Bucks* newly fitted with double chimney, 17 June 1958.
(MLS Collection/ G Shuttleworth)

1004 *County* of *Somerset* at Swindon shed alongside 'Castle' 5062 *Earl of Shaftesbury*, 16 June 1957.
(R.C. Riley)

Shrewsbury's 1013 *County of Dorset* at its home depot alongside 5936 *Oakley Hall,* 17 September 1958. (J. Hodge)

1022 *County of Northampton* on the turntable at Cardiff Canton, 31 January 1959. The tender has been filled with a load of decent coal to supplement the ovoids visible at the back of the tender. (J. Hodge)

1003 *County* of Wilts
at Newton Abbot shed,
19 July 1958.
(R.C. Riley)

1005 *County* of Devon
being prepared on
Canton shed ready to
haul the 12.32 Cardiff-
Penzance as far as
Plymouth, 28 November
1959. Canton's own
6935 *Browsholme Hall*
stands behind. 1005 has
been fitted with a four
row superheater (note
the second 'box' below
the handrail on the
smokebox).
(J. Hodge)

1016 *County* of Hants
at Canton shed with
one of the depot's own
'Castles' in the distance,
27 August 1961.
(J. Hodge)

1013 *County* of Dorset with steam to spare on Shrewsbury shed, c1960. (GW Trust)

Shrewsbury's 1016 *County of Hants,* now with 4-row superheat boiler, backs into Newton Abbot shed after being coaled with ovoids ready for its return the next day on the 8am Plymouth, the shared Newton Abbot/Shrewsbury double home working normally covered by the two depot's top link 'Castles'. Ovoids were not the best fuel for this tough duty. (GW Trust)

1023 *County* of *Oxford* of Swindon, for many years the only 'County' based at Truro, and displaced only after full dieselisation west of Plymouth, ready to leave Cardiff Canton shed on a train for the West of England, May 1961. (J. Hodge)

1022 *County* of *Northampton* during overhaul at Swindon Works alongside D63XX diesel hydraulics destined for Laira diesel depot, 1961.
(GW Trust/N. Preedy)

1006 *County* of *Cornwall* with 4-row superheater boiler, at Laira, 29 April 1962.
(GW Trust)

The 'Counties' suffered from the decision to dieselise the Western Region first and all had been withdrawn by November 1964, the last survivor being 1011 *County of Chester,* which had its smokebox door numberplate removed and the numerals 1011 stencilled on the bufferbeam for the last few weeks when it operated some special trains. None of the engines reached a million miles in traffic – the highest mileage of 794,555 miles being accumulated by 1012, withdrawn in April 1964. They were survived not only by many of the 1946-50 built 'Castles', but even by some of those built in the 1920s.

1013 *County* of *Dorset* emerges from Stafford Road depot in a swathe of steam towards the end of the duties of 'Counties' north of Wolverhampton, c1963.
(GW Trust)

1011 *County* of *Chester,* the last survivor of the 'County' class, standing at Swindon ready to haul a 'farewell' railtour organised by the Stephenson Locomotive Society, September 1964. 1011 was withdrawn in November 1964 making the class extinct.
(GW Trust)

1029 *County of Worcester*, deprived of all identity and rusting in the company of a 'Hall' and pannier tank at Swindon, 1963.
(GW Trust)

The last one in service, 1011 *County of Chester*, now withdrawn and stored awaiting disposal, recognizable only by the number painted on the bufferbeam, inscribed for the SLS railtour, January 1965.
(GW Trust)

The distinctive nameplate of the 'County' class, 1011 *County of Chester.*
(GW Trust)

allocated to the main depots of Old Oak Common (six engines) and Bristol Bath Road (six also). 1001 at Newton Abbot and 1004, 1006 and 1009 at Plymouth Laira suggested that working expresses in Devon and Cornwall might be important also. Further allocations to Newton Abbot (1018 and 1019) and to Wolverhampton Stafford Road (1016 and 1017) widened their sphere of operation to where perhaps they would be most suitable, but it was on the main line from Paddington to Bristol that they were first judged and found wanting.

As one of the first new designs to appear after the war, they aroused the interest of the railway press, especially as they appeared to depart significantly from Churchward's standards

The prototype 1000 *County of Middlesex* (already looking travel-stained despite being less than twelve months old) near Brentham Halt between Greenford and Park Royal with the 11.40 Birkenhead-Paddington, 25 June 1946.
(J. Hodge Collection)

Operation

Hawksworth's 'Counties' inauguration onto the Great Western scene in 1946 was blighted by the railways' rundown at the end of the Second World War. Coal supplies were scarce and of poor quality. Skilled maintenance staff were still in short supply and the rest of the GW locomotive fleet was suffering from overuse during the war and needed priority for restoration to adequate standards. Despite their power with their high pressure boilers, with 6ft 3in driving wheels they were a compromise between the GW's express and mixed traffic engines and are reputed to have been designed for the more heavily graded of the railway's routes – west of Newton Abbot, the North & West and the northern route above Wolverhampton. However, the early allocation of the 'Counties' belied this, the initial series all being

1009, still unnamed but named *County of Carmarthen* in 1948, in a filthy state on the summer 11.50am Paignton-Wolverhampton, with a motley mixture of GW and LMS stock near Flax Bourton, August 1946. The chalked 100 on the smokebox under the route identification numerals indicated that its previous working was the 5.30am Paddington-Plymouth via Bristol.
(GW Trust)

and particularly because of their high boiler pressure. Many correspondents were sending reports to Cecil J. Allen for his columns in the *Railway Magazine* and expressing disappointment. The prototype, 1000, with its massive double chimney started work between Paddington and Wolverhampton before moving later to Newton Abbot, but it was on the level Paddington-Bristol route that their early work was noted and it was very undistinguished. As early as February 1946 there was an account of 1002, admittedly with a heavy load (fourteen coaches) losing time steadily all the way to Bath on the 1.15pm Paddington-Bristol, with speed dribbling away to just 48mph on the slightly rising gradients between Didcot and Swindon. Of course, loads were heavy with express train frequency still limited as recovery from war conditions took place.

1004, still unnamed – it received the name *County of Somerset* in August 1946 – passing Iver station on the 7am Plymouth-Paddington, Spring 1946. Photos of 'Counties' in their first year of existence demonstrate a distinct shortage of cleaners with many men not yet demobbed from the armed forces.
(GW Trust)

In the October 1946 *Railway Magazine*, Cecil J. Allen devoted much of his article to the performance (or lack of it) of the new 'Counties', the first twenty of which had been delivered and were operating by then. Despite receiving many logs, Allen stated that few were of merit, although flashes of brilliance were perceived. However, most runs appeared sluggish, with the 'Counties' in trouble for steam. A run with an unidentified 'County' on the 9.10am Paddington-Wolverhampton, admittedly with a heavy 15- coach 525 ton gross load train was instanced as an example. The train was already nine minutes late from High Wycombe where the recorder joined the train, but

at first the run looked promising with 45mph sustained on the climb to Saunderton summit. The engine appeared winded, however, and barely reached 70mph on the descent, and dropped to 40mph on the 1 in 200 climb to Ardley. 70mph at Fosse Road was again maximum before Leamington, but the climb to Hatton with this load was very respectable, with the summit topped at 35mph. However, the train was steadily losing time all the way, and despite being unchecked, was twenty minutes late into Wolverhampton where engines were changed.

A better run on the 9am relief to the 9.10 was recorded with 1016,

a Stafford Road engine, with ten coaches, 340 tons gross. The early part of the run to Saunderton was spoiled by signal checks, but 1016 touched 80mph at Ashendon Junction, surmounted Ardley at 54 and after slowing to 45mph through Leamington station, sustained 48mph on Hatton Bank. Most of the reports, however, came from experiences on the Bristol road. A regular traveller from Bath to Paddington and back sent details of several 'County' runs, most poor. The 'best of a bad bunch' as expressed by the recorder, was 1008 on the down 6.30pm Paddington-Plymouth via Bristol. It had twelve coaches, 405 tons gross and started

very sluggishly, only attaining 49mph by Southall. 54-58mph on the level between Slough and Maidenhead was below par, but the engine perked up slightly after Reading to average 60mph from Reading to Swindon, 74 was touched momentarily in the descent of Dauntsey Bank and arrival at Chippenham was five minutes late, with the net time exactly as scheduled. And that was his best!

Cecil J. Allen returned to the subject again in August 1947, when the engines had overcome, hopefully, their teething problems, though trouble with poor coal was still evident. One bitter winter day (the 1947 winter was notorious for the long spell of arctic conditions) 1026, one of the second batch of ten built in early 1947, left Bath 34 minutes late with a 12-coach 435 ton gross load, climbed through Box at 52½mph, fell from 60 to 50 on Dauntsey but then ran into real operating problems and eventually arrived in London 97 minutes late. 1028 of Bristol Bath Road on a train leaving Chippenham at 12.44pm, with thirteen coaches (470 tons gross) fell from 53½ to 40mph at Dauntsey and got up to 71mph after Swindon, but had fallen to 58mph by Reading, recovered to 66mph after Slough and ran the 92 miles in 98 minutes net, satisfactory but hardly up to the standards of 'Castles' at the time. The problem was that the authorities appeared to be treating them as alternatives to 'Castles' on the GW main lines and in BR power category terms, they were 6MT rather than 7P engines. The engines were reported as having trouble maintaining pressure above 230-250lbs psi – the double-chimneyed 1000 was said to show no advantage.

1016 *County* of Hants near Wrexham during the arctic winter of 1947 with a Birkenhead – Paddington service, 1 March 1947.
(GW Trust/J.G. Jefferson)

1000 *County* of *Middlesex* backs onto Bath Road shed after arriving from Paddington, 'Castle' 5077 *Fairey Battle* having taken over for the run on to Plymouth, looking in no better condition, c1947. A Collett built '4575' small prairie tank is on shed in the background.
(J.M. Bentley Collection)

Unnamed 1001 (named *County of Bucks* in December 1947) runs into St Erth station with the 1.55pm stopping train from Penzance to Plymouth, 3 October 1947.
(MLS Collection/J.D. Darby)

1018, *County of Leicester,* with steam to spare on this occasion, climbing unaided to Dainton summit with a Wolverhampton – Penzance express, August 1947. The front vehicle is a GW 'Centenary' Brake coach.
(MLS Collection/J.D. Darby)

One better run was recorded between Taunton and Exeter on a Paddington-Plymouth train in October 1947:

Taunton – Exeter, October 1947
1015 *County of Gloucester* (Old Oak Common)
11 chs, 350/380 tons

Distance Miles	Location	Time mins secs	Speed mph
0.0	Taunton	00.00	
2.0	Norton Fitzwarren	04.02	
5.7	Poole Sidings	08.08	51
7.1	Wellington	09.35	56
9.9	MP 173	12.53	42½
10.9	Whiteball	14.24	39½
15.9	Tiverton Junction	19.30	68 / 64
18.2	Collumpton	21.30	69
22.4	Hele	25.16	66½
27.4	Stoke Canon	29.55	59/ sigs stand
30.8	Exeter	35.59 (34 net)	

In this same article in December 1947 Cecil J. Allen conjectured at length about their strengths and weaknesses and concluded that they needed different driving methods to the 'Stars', 'Castles' and 'Kings', which traditionally ran with wide open regulator and short cut-off. The 'Counties' appeared to go better on partly opened regulator and longer cut-off, and for some reason their firing seemed to be trickier than the four-cylinder engines. He concluded that they were happier on undulating routes where power was needed in short bursts and that they were therefore best in areas like Devon and Cornwall rather than competing with 'Kings' and 'Castles' on Brunel's 'billiard table' routes.

Cecil J. Allen was determined to see for himself and in September 1947 he acquired a footplate pass to travel on 'Counties' on a number of routes. He commenced his own trials with a run on 1006 *County of Cornwall* (appropriately), a Laira engine, on the up *Cornish Riviera Express* from Penzance to Plymouth.

Penzance – Plymouth, September 1947
1006 *County of Cornwall* (Laira)
9 chs 293/315 tons
Driver Hocking, Fireman Rogers (Laira)

Distance Miles	Location	Time mins secs	Speed mph	Schedule		Working
0.0	Penzance	00.00		T		
1.9	Marazion	04.20	43½ / 34½		1 in 86R	23% cut-off/ just 2nd port
5.6	St Erth	10.12		1¼ L		
0.0		00.00				
1.6	Hayle	02.58	40/25½		1 in 61R	33% cut-off /full reg.
5.6	Gwinear Road	09.51		T		
0.0		00.00				
2.5	Cambourne	05.08	41/25		1 in 61R	35% cut-off, 280 psi
4.1	Carn Brea	08.07	50			
6.2	Redruth	10.53	35*			
8.3	Scorrier	13.53	56½			23% cut-off/ 1st port
10.0	Chacewater	15.52	45*/61		1 in 80F	
15.2	Truro	22.34		1½ E		
0.0		00.00		T		
1.8	MP 299	04.17	24½		1 in 78R	
5.3	Probus	08.23	57			
6.8	MP 294	10.53	53			
7.6	Grampound Road	12.11	27	½ L	1 in 67R	30% cut-off, 230 psi
9.3	MP 291½	14.25	53			
12.1	Burngullow	18.39	36		1 in 70R	
14.5	St Austell	21.39		1 E		
19.0	Par	27.13		1¾ E		250lbs psi
0.0		00.00		T		
2.1	MP 279¾	05.41	22½ / pws		1 in 62R	
4.4	Lostwithiel	09.41	25*			
7.8	Bodmin Road	15.18	44	2¼ L		
13.6	Doublebois	26.54	39/28/24½ /29		1 in 67/70R	32% cut-off, 260 psi
		-	27/29		1 in 90R	35% cut-off
16.9	Liskeard	31.18	56	2¼ L		
20.0	Menheniot	35.27				
25.4	St Germans	41.44	45*/25*			
30.5	Saltash	49.05	15*			
31.6	St Budeaux	52.08	sigs			
33.5	Devonport	54.49				
34.7	Plymouth North Rd	58.00		1 L		

Cecil J. Allen reported that in his view the engine was master of the job, sure-footed (as all GW engines), with pressure fluctuating around 230-250lbs psi most of the way, the engine being driven mainly on first valve of the regulator and 25-30% cut-off except on the steepest gradients where full regulator was used.

A footplate run on the same train timed by Ronald Nelson and described in his book *Locomotive Performance – A Footplate Survey* (Ian Allan 1979) is a bit of a puzzle. The load was slightly heavier – nine coaches for 314/330 tons – and he'd gone down overnight with the Paddington sleeper hauled by 1012 *County of Denbigh*, which had lost time in Cornwall because of poor

steaming. 1012 was booked to return to Plymouth with the up *Cornish Riviera* with Inspector Vercoe and a Laira crew and Ronald Nelson made the comment that the engine could not be worked as hard as it might have been because of its indifferent steaming. However, it beat all start-to-stop times in Cornwall achieved by 1006 above, apparently by the expert judgment of driver Porter and the inspector. Use of the injector immediately reduced boiler pressure, but the undulating nature of the route allowed recovery. Much of the run was made on 1st valve and 25% cut-off. The first time full regulator was used was on the 1 in 70 climb to Burngullow mounted at 44mph compared with 36mph

with 1006, and then from Bodmin Road on the long 1 in 67/70 to Doublebois, opening up to 35% cut-off and holding 29/30mph, again slightly superior to 1006, but with steam pressure dropping rapidly from 260lbs psi at Par to slightly under 190lbs at the summit. Despite the problems, the train arrived at Plymouth North Road four minutes early.

Cecil J. Allen continued on the 1.56pm Plymouth-Paddington as far as Newton Abbot, for which a 'County ' had also been specially rostered, which worked without a pilot, the nine coach load of 315 tons gross being the maximum allowed for a single 'County' or 'Castle' over the South Devon banks.

Plymouth North Road-Newton Abbot, September 1947
1.56pm Plymouth-Paddington
1028 *County of Warwick* (Bristol Bath Road)
9 chs, 301/315 tons
Laira driver & fireman

Distance Miles	Location	Time mins secs	Speed mph	Schedule		Working
0.0	Plymouth North Rd	00.00		T		
1.5	Lipson Jcn	04.03		T		
2.8	Tavistock Jcn	05.53				
4.0	Plympton	07.06	55			
		-	48/27		I in 42R	35% cut-off
6.7	Hemerdon	14.41	16/9	¼ E		50% cut-off
8.4	Cornwood	17.39				pws 20*
10.8	Ivybridge	21.58				230 lbs psi
14.1	Wrangaton	26.39	42			
16.3	Brent	29.24	-	½ L		
18.6	Rattery	32.01	56½	T		
23.1	Totnes	37.15	50*	1¼ E		30% cut-off
28.0	Dainton	44.53	38/15		1 in 65/38R	40% cut-off (last mile)
30.8	Aller Jcn	49.48				
31.9	Newton Abbot	52.00		2 E		

Cecil J. Allen commented that the driver left dropping the cut-off and opening right up too late on both Hemerdon and Dainton

inclines, until speed had fallen significantly and then just crawled over the summits – luckily the weather was dry and there was no

slipping. However, despite this, the schedule was slack and the run was completed a couple of minutes early.

1018 *County* of *Leicester* leaving Teignmouth with an up express, 1 June 1949.
(Colour Rail/E.D. Bruton)

1012 *County* of *Denbigh* passing Iver on a Kingswear-Paddington summer Saturday express with a LMS and then a pre-grouping Midland coach next to the engine, another LMS coach fifth, 30 August 1947.
(GW Trust)

1013 *County* of *Dorset* passing Hockley between Wolverhampton and Birmingham with an up express composed of an extraordinary array of unusual GW coaches – second from the engine, an early Collett corridor coach, then a GW 'excursion' coach, fourth is a 'centenary' brake, then a row of ocean liner saloons, 19 October 1947.
(GW Trust)

1000 *County* of *Middlesex* passes Newbury with a down West of England express, passing a GW twin railcar (No.38 with a Collett coach sandwiched between the power cars) on the far platform and a MS&WJR 2-4-0 survivor in the down platform, 16 April 1948.
(GW Trust)

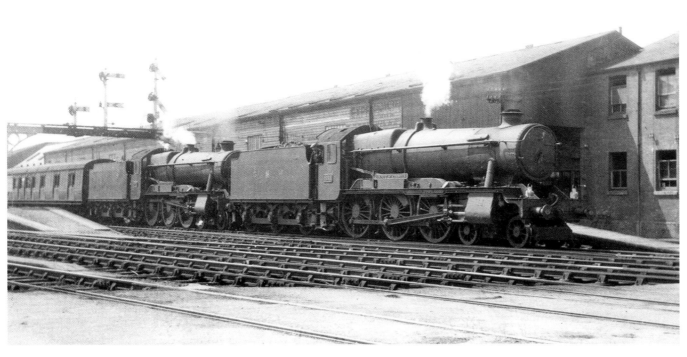

1011 *County* of *Chester* and 1028 *County of Warwick* double-head an up West of England express at Exeter St David's, 27 July 1948. (GW Trust)

1005 *County* of *Devon* rounds the sea wall and enters Teignmouth station with an Exeter – Newton Abbot stopping train, c1948. (J.M. Bentley Collection)

His third run the next day, after overnighting in Newton Abbot, was on the through Plymouth-Shrewsbury double-home diagram with Newton Abbot and Shrewsbury engines and crew alternate days. These turns were normally the preserve of carefully selected 'Castles' which stayed on the job usually for three months until due for the first valve & piston examination and exchange after Swindon Works overhaul. Allen travelled from Newton Abbot at 9.46am with the Shrewsbury men, and instead of a Shrewsbury 'Castle' one of the Laira 'Counties', 1022, had been rostered for the occasion. The run around the sea coast was somewhat sluggish – the train stopped at both Teignmouth and Dawlish and Inspector Pullen found the lubrication pipes blocked and cleared them during the Exeter stop. Cecil J. Allen therefore did not start timing until leaving Exeter.

Exeter – Bristol Temple Meads, September 1947
9.46 Newton Abbot – Shrewsbury – Liverpool
1022 *County of Northampton* **(Laira)**
13 chs, 408/440 tons
Shrewsbury crew

Distance Miles	Location	Times mins secs	Speed mph	Schedule
0.0	Exeter	00.00		T
3.4	Stoke Canon	07.11	43½	
7.2	Silverton	12.08	53	
12.6	Collumpton	18.04	57½	
14.9	Tiverton Jcn	20.44	48/55	
19.2	Burlescombe	25.59	44	
19.9	Whiteball	27.06	37½	
23.7	Wellington	30.58	77½	
28.8	Norton Fitzwarren	35.02	76	
30.8	Taunton	38.11		¼ L
0.0		00.00		T
2.4	Creech Jcn	04.25		½ L
4.8	Cogload Jcn	07.01	57	
8.0	Fordgate	10.16	66	
11.6	Bridgwater	14.22		½ E
0.0		00.00		T
2.5	Dunball	04.42	53	
6.3	Highbridge	08.49	60	¼ E
9.0	Brent Knoll	11.36		
13.0	Bleadon	15.04	70½	
13.5	Uphill Jcn	15.52	20*	1 E
14.8	Weston –s-Mare	19.50		1¼ E
0.0		00.00		T
2.6	Worle Jcn	04.18	25*	¾ E
3.8	Puxton	06.31		
7.4	Yatton	10.55	57	
11.3	Nailsea	15.02	59	
13.5	Flax Bourton	17.30		
17.6	Parson Street	22.23	40*	
18.4	Bedminster	23.48	sigs*	
19.4	Bristol Temple Meads	26.46		¾ L

He commented that the driver, who had not driven a 'County' before, received several tips from Inspector Pullen who was accompanying the footplate guest. After the early lubrication problems, there was no more trouble although 1022 was slow away from Exeter. At the suggestion of the inspector, the driver varied cut-off between 25-35% with first valve of the regulator. Steam pressure was 270lbs psi on departure from Exeter, fell to 250 at Whiteball and further to 240 north of Highbridge.

Cecil J. Allen commented that the footplate crew experienced considerable vibration when they were travelling at 70mph – being a 2-cylinder engine, it did not ride as smoothly as a 'King' or 'Castle'.

After two years' experience of the engines, further 'Counties' were sent to the West of England. Truro received its first (1023), Exeter got one (1020 from Chester) and two were allocated to Penzance (1019 and 1022). On receipt of the whole thirty of the class, eight were at Old Oak, seven at Bristol Bath Road, six at Laira (reduced to three as the Truro, Exeter and one of the Newton Abbot allocation were from Laira), three at Newton Abbot (reduced to two on transfer of 1019 to Penzance). Stafford Road had five primarily for working north of Wolverhampton and one final odd one out (1027) was allocated to Westbury.

In December 1949, Cecil J. Allen wrote an article on 'Western Locomotive Work' for the current *Trains Illustrated Magazine.* After covering noteworthy performances of 'Kings' and 'Castles' he turned to the 'Counties' and commented:

'Some of the more enterprising drivers are coaxing some remarkable work out of them. When I did some riding on 'County' footplates a couple of years ago, I found drivers reluctant to 'pull them up' to anything less than 25% cut-off, and never did I see the main port of the regulator anything like fully open except when climbing really steep banks, like those of Cornwall and South Devon. The engines seemed happier too on steeply

1014 *County* of *Glamorgan,* newly overhauled and with 'British Railways' inscribed on the tender in GW style, surmounts the 1in 100 gradient at Church Stretton with the 1.35pm Sunday Shrewsbury-Bristol express composed of LMS rolling stock, 11 July 1948.
(MLS Collection/J.D. Darby)

1024 *County* of *Pembroke* passes Chester Racecourse with a Chester-Shrewsbury stopping train, c1949.
(MLS Collection)

1024 *County* of Pembroke pauses at Leamington Spa with a Wolverhampton-Paddington express, July 1948.
(J.M. Bentley Collection/G. Coltas)

1013 *County* of *Dorset* passes between the Dawlish tunnels with a train for the Midlands, c1949.
(J.M. Bentley Collection)

1018 *County* of *Leicester* descending Rattery bank with a stopping train from Plymouth to Newton Abbot and Exeter, 4 February 1951.
(GW Trust)

up-and-down lines than on long stretches of level running. Much has happened in the ensuing two years, however, and now the 'Counties', despite wheels of 6ft 3in diameter ... frequently get over the ground at sustained speeds not far from those of the 'Castles' and 'Kings'.'

He then illustrated his point with logs of a couple of runs, both made at different times and routes by the same engine, 1026 *County of Salop*. First, he quotes a run logged by my friend, George Carpenter, when 1026 came up from Oxford to Paddington with a 11-coach 370 ton gross load, completing the 27.5 miles to Reading in 30 minutes 31 seconds start-to-stop with running in the low 70s from Goring to Tilehurst. Then it tore out of Reading passing Maidenhead in 12 minutes 47 seconds attaining 73mph before signal checks intervened. What was noteworthy, said Allen, was the driver was working with full regulator and 18% cut-off, just as he would have driven a 'Castle'.

The second run was with a much lighter load, just seven coaches for 225 tons gross, but the 'County ' ran from Bristol to Bridgwater start-to-stop in 30 minutes 57 seconds for the 33 miles averaging exactly 72mph over the twenty five miles between Flax Bourton and Dunball with a maximum of 76½mph between Nailsea and Yatton. The train had apparently left Bath fourteen minutes late, and Bristol ten late. After being held at Bridgwater for five minutes, it gained just over another four minutes on to Taunton, arriving

1019 *County of Merioneth* crosses the Tamar into Cornwall at Saltash with a holiday Midlands-Penzance express formed of LMS coaches, 28 July 1951. (MLS Collection)

1022 *County of Northampton* leaving Penzance with the 8.05am London train which it will power as far as Plymouth, July 1951. The meaning of the chalked inscriptions on the smokebox door is obscure and does not refer to the train currently being hauled. (GW Trust)

there two minutes early. This was exceptional speedy running in 1949.

O.S. Nock had a footplate run on a 'County' in Cornwall with the doyen of the class, 1000 *County of Middlesex* also on the *Cornish Riviera Express,* but in the down direction. The load was eight coaches, 272/290 tons, the date 23 October 1952. The train departed Plymouth three minutes late and ran the 34.7 miles to first stop Par in 54 minutes exactly dropping just two minutes due to a p-way slowing at Liskeard. The engine was worked hard – 35% cut-off and full regulator – to maintain 28mph on the 1 in 78/68 after St Germans, but maintained its full steam pressure of 280lbs. Par to Truro (19 miles) took 29 minutes, 35 seconds, holding time exactly, with 31 mph, falling to 24½ on the steepest 1 in 61 grades to St Austell

(38% cut-off and full regulator) and 29/27½ mph as the gradient eased to 1 in 90 before Burngullow. Nock noted that the fireman maintained full steam pressure despite the hard work. He also noted that 1000 had used 2,100 gallons of its 4,000 gallon capacity tender (39 gallons per mile). The climb out of Par up to Chacewater (1 in 80) brought the steam pressure down to 255lbs psi, but after that the hard work was complete and running in the forties with a maximum of 54mph after Redruth gained a minute and the smart station work at Truro, Gwinear Road and St Erth enabled the *Cornish Riviera Express* to terminate one minute early in Penzance, after a final 60mph dash down the 1 in 60 from Gwinear Road. O.S. Nock noted 1,250 gallons of water remained in the tender

giving an average consumption of 34.4 gallons per mile for the eighty mile run, indicating the easier working of the engine after Truro, with the fireman allowing the pressure to drop to 235lbs psi. Nock was impressed at the exact nature of the timekeeping, but it must be noted that most of the gain was due to station staff cutting the generous station allowances and the 'County' seemed to have little in hand on the schedule.

O.S. Nock in his book *British Locomotives from the Footplate,* published in 1950, describes a footplate run with Bristol Bath Road's 1014 *County of Glamorgan* on the 9am Bristol-Paddington allowed virtually two hours for the 106.9 miles up from Bath. It was heavily delayed east of Didcot, but with 13 coaches 470 tons gross, ran well to that point.

Bath-Didcot (pass), 1949
9am Bristol-Paddington
1014 *County of Glamorgan* 82A
13 chs 432/470 tons
Driver Leonard, Fireman Burge (82A)

Distance Miles	Location	Times mins secs	Speed mph	Working	Punctuality
0.0	Bath	00.00			1 L
2.3	Bathampton	04.27	46	35% cut-off	
5.0	Box	07.50	52	1st port	
7.9	MP 99	12.03	32 ½ /34 ½	Main valve	
12.9	Chippenham	17.52	64	30%, 1st valve	1 L
19.2	Dauntsey	23.39	68 / 64 ½	25%	
21.6	Incline Box	26.11	50 ½	30%, Main valve	
24.0	Wootton Bassett	28.53	56 ½	25%	
29.6	Swindon	34.35	65		1 ½ E
35.3	Shrivenham	39.46	67 ½	250-270lbs psi	
40.4	Uffington	44.16	69 ½		
43.0	Challow	46.30	71 ½		
46.5	Wantage Road	49.27	72		
50.4	Steventon	52.46	70 ½		4 ¼ E
53.8	Didcot	55.40	70 ½		4 ¾ E

The inspector had advised Nock of p-way slacks at Reading and Slough and that they would try to get sufficient time in hand, but signal checks at Goring before and after Slough and outside Paddington station made the train 13¾ minutes late in. Water consumption was around 40 gallons per mile and coal consumption was described as 'moderate'. 1014 returned on the 1.15pm Paddington-Bristol with a gross load of 415 tons, but the coal was poor including 'ovoids' and there were a succession of checks all the way to Reading. West of Swindon the crew attempted to regain some time, accelerating to 66mph before the descent of Dauntsey Bank where 79mph was reached, sustaining 72mph before the Bath stop, covering the 29.6 miles from Swindon to Bath in 28 ¼ minutes pass-to-stop. The net time from Paddington was 108 minutes. Nock comments that the engine rode smoothly, in contrast to other footplate passengers later who found the 'Counties' could be rough with much vibration.

1027 *County of Stafford* hurries a Swansea-Cardiff two coach stopping passenger train plus an assortment of parcels vans into Llantrisant station, between Bridgend and Cardiff, May 1951.
(GW Trust/R.C. Riley)

1017 *County of Hereford* at Saltney Junction, with the Wolverhampton-Chester leg of a Paddington-Birkenhead express, c1951. (GW Trust)

In the early days, some of the 'Counties'' best work was performed north of Wolverhampton with very substantial trains. Later most Paddington-Birkenhead expresses shed their restaurant car portions at Wolverhampton so six-seven coach trains then became the norm, but O.S. Nock in his book *Fifty Years of Western Express Running* (Edward Everard Ltd, 1954) tabled a number of runs with thirteen-coach loads.

Wolverhampton – Wellington

Distance Miles	Location	1029 *County of Worcester* 427/460 tons Driver Chester (84A)			1025 *County of Radnor* 429/460 tons Driver Griffiths (84A)		1029 *County of Worcester* 458/500 tons Driver Shaw (84A)	
		Times mins secs	Speed mph		Times mins secs	Speed mph	Times mins secs	Speed mph
0.0	Wolverhampton	00.00			00.00		00.00	
1.3	Stafford Rd Jcn	03.20		1 in 100F	03.01		03.11	
4.7	Codsall	07.05	62	1 in 242R	06.51	61½	07.09	58
7.7	Albrighton	09.58		1 in 100F	09.42		10.04	
9.2	Cosford	11.10	80	1 in 137F	10.55	78	11.21	73½
12.5	Shifnal	13.51		1 in 150R	13.36		14.10	
15.4	Hollinswood Box	17.35	41	1 in 100R	17.00	43	17.45	43
16.6	Oakengates	19.03			18.24	sigs	19.13	
19.6	Wellington	22.25			22.52		23.16	

1029's run with 500 tons was particularly noteworthy for its exceptional climb to Hollinswood (1.8 miles at 1 in 150, followed by 2.8 miles at 1 in 100) when Nock calculated that it was developing 1,500 drawbar horsepower. In *Four Thousand Miles on the Footplate* (Ian Allan 1952) Nock describes a potentially even better run with 1016 *County of Hants* when Stafford Road driver, Bert Griffiths had a gross load of 500 tons and was driven very hard to recover earlier delays. After a maximum of 73mph at Cosford, 1016 was opened right out falling to 49mph a mile short of Hollinswood summit. However, the cylinders were beating the boiler, pressure dropped to 210lbs psi and speed fell to 38½ mph at the top of the bank. Easing down to Wellington immediately allowed steam pressure to recover fully. Nock comments that Griffiths deliberately 'mortgaged' the boiler to produce maximum output for a short distance and commented that whilst 2,000 indicated horsepower had been calculated for this effort, the power was momentary only. Nock compared the experience on the footplate of a 'Castle' worked similarly hard and said that whilst the 'Castle' purred (sic), the 'County' began 'quivering like a live thing'. The vibration was very noticeable.

Southbound runs over the same section were also tabled with a number of 'Counties', with 1025 and 1029 featuring again with the locally allocated 1017. In this direction, the engines face a four mile climb out of Wellington at 1 in 132/220 to Hollinswood and after the five mile descent, another four mile climb at 1 in 137/100 to the summit beyond Albrighton.

Wellington – Wolverhampton (Up *Zulu*)

Distance Miles	Location	1025 *County of Radnor* 417/445 tons Driver Griffiths (84A)		1017 *County of Hereford* 727/455 tons Driver Griffiths (84A)		1029 *County of Worcester* 459/500 tons Driver MacMillan (84A)	
		Times mins seccs	Speed mph	Times mins secs	Speed mph	Times mins secs	Speed mph
0.0	Wellington	00.00		00.00		00.00	
3.0	Oakengates	06.35		06.14		06.32	
4.2	Hollinswood Box	08.37	34	08.03	37½	08.29	35½
7.1	Shifnal	12.02		11.44		11.45	
10.4	Cosford	14.48	73½	14.34	72	14.23	77½
11.9	Albrighton	16.12		15.56		15.42	
13.4	MP 148	17.50	50	17.31	53	17.21	50
14.9	Codsall	19.28	59	19.06	63	18.57	
19.6	Wolverhampton	25.59		26.00	pws	25.22	

All of these runs in both directions were carried out by the exceptionally competent drivers in Stafford Road's No.2 link.

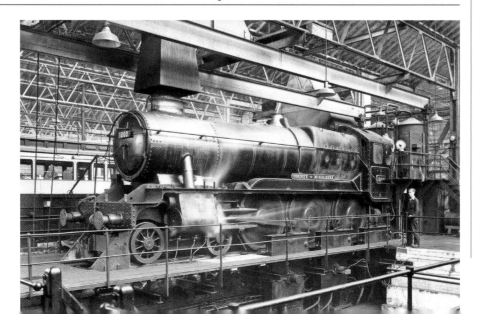

In 1952 1000 *County of Middlesex* was put through a number of tests to try to improve its performance and that of its sister locomotives. Here it is at speed on the rollers in Swindon Works, 1952. (GW Trust)

1000 *County* of *Middlesex* on a trial run with a heavy 13-coach plus dynamometer car between Wootton Bassett and Badminton, 1952. It is fitted with an indicator shelter so that Swindon testing staff can take measurements from the engine at speed protected by the shelter.
(GW Trust)

1024 *County* of *Pembroke* leans to the curve at Lostwithiel with the up *Cornish Riviera Express*, 4 July 1952.
(GW Trust/T.C. Cole)

1006 *County* of *Cornwall* on the Paddington-Bristol *Bristolian* passing Bath's Sydney Gardens before its acceleration to the 105 minute non-stop timing and its haulage by 'Kings', then later 'Castles'. No 'County' is known to have been used on the 105 or 100 minute *Bristolian*, 8 September 1952. (GW Trust)

1019 *County* of *Merioneth* at Little Somerford with an Easter excursion to South Wales, c1952.
(GW Trust)

1028 *County* of *Warwick* on the 6.30am Paignton to the West Midlands on a summer Saturday in 1952.
(GW Trust)

Penzance allocated
1004 *County of Somerset* leaves Bristol Temple Meads with a stopping train for Exeter, c1953.
(J.M. Bentley Collection/ G. Coltas)

1004 *County of Somerset* climbing Fishponds bank, the Midland route out of Bristol, with the *Cornishman,* banked by an LMS 4F 0-6-0, 44149, 6 August 1953.
(GW Trust)

1005 *County* of Devon on a Swindon-Bristol via Badminton stopping train is admired by a small boy and his dad at Chipping Sodbury station, c1953. (J.M. Bentley Collection)

1005 *County* of Devon between Teignmouth and Dawlish on a heavy 13-coach summer Saturday train from South Devon to the North West, c1953. (MLS Collection)

1008 *County* of Cardigan enters Birmingham Snow Hill with the daily Birkenhead-Bournemouth through train, 1953.
(GW Trust)

1028 *County* of Warwick passes Stoke Gifford marshalling yard with a Bristol-Paddington express, 8 October 1953.
(GW Trust)

1003 *County* of *Wilts* crosses Broadstone Viaduct with a Liverpool-Kingswear express, 26 April 1954. (G.W. Trust/J.T. Whitnall)

1004 *County* of *Somerset* enters Paddington with the 8am from Kingswear, 14 August 1954. (GW Trust)

1006 *County* of *Cornwall* passing Aller Junction with what appears to be two coaches for Plymouth off a train that has divided at Newton Abbot, the main train going to Kingswear, 1954. (J.M. Bentley Collection)

1012 *County* of *Denbigh* running in after overhaul at Swindon on a Swindon-Bristol stopping train, August 1954. (J.M. Bentley Collection)

1024 *County* of *Pembroke* at Plymouth North Road with an up fitted freight, 1954.
(J.M. Bentley Collection)

1025 *County* of *Radnor* departs from Chester past Saltney Junction with the 5.50pm Chester-Ruabon commuter service, 8 September 1954.
(GW Trust)

1006 *County* of *Cornwall* runs into Liskeard station with a Truro-Plymouth stopping train, 1955.
(GW Trust)

1018 *County* of *Leicester* with the 6.20pm Penzance-Kensington milk train near Par, 9 July 1955.
(GW Trust)

1018 *County of Leicester* passes through Par with a class 'H' unfitted freight, April 1955.
(J.M. Bentley Collection/Photomatic)

1025 *County of Radnor*, still in black livery and single-chimneyed, with a down Plymouth express from the West Midlands at Powderham, near Exeter, 1 May 1955.
(Colour Rail)

1025 *County* of *Radnor* leaves Pontypool Road station with the through 9.05am Liverpool-Plymouth express, c1955.
(J. Hodge)

1026 *County* of *Salop* climbs Filton Bank with a North & West express for Shrewsbury and Crewe, c1955.
(J.M. Bentley Collection/ G. Heiron)

1028 *County* of *Warwick* wheels a freight through Oxford towards Hinksey Yard and Didcot, with a Southern Bulleid light pacific waiting to take over a cross-country train for Bournemouth and a LNWR G2 0-8-0 in the sidings obscured by the 'County', c1955.
(MLS Collection)

1029 *County of Worcester* with the 4.35pm Neyland-Paddington parcels train passing through Whitland, 24 June 1955. (GW Trust)

1015 *County of Gloucester* arrives at Plymouth North Road with the *Cornishman* from Penzance, c1955. (GW Trust)

1018 *County* of *Leicester* pilots 6023 *King Edward II* over the South Devon banks and coasts through Totnes before tackling the climb to Dainton with a London bound express, c1955.
(GW Trust)

Truro's lone 'County', 1023 *County of Oxford* blasts out of Torquay up the 1 in 55 gradient through Torre with the 8.55am to Paddington, c1955.
(GW Trust/Peter Gray)

1023 *County of Oxford* accelerates from Penzance through Marazion with a train for Plymouth and points east, c1955.
(GW Trust)

1002 *County* of Berks still in black and single-chimneyed with a down express for Plymouth and Penzance at Twyford, 1 April 1956.
(Colour Rail/T. Owen)

1028 *County* of *Warwick* at Exeter St David's with the 7.45am Paignton-Newcastle formed of LMS carriage stock, c1955.
(GW Trust)

A side view of 1024 *County of Pembroke* at speed, c1955.
(GW Trust)

1018 *County* of *Leicester* on a milk train at Camborne, July 1956. (R.C. Riley)

1021 *County* of *Montgomery* attaches two through vehicles from Millbay Docks to the 11am Penzance-Paddington at Exeter St David's, 31 March 1956. (GW Trust)

1012 *County* of Denbigh leaves Par with the *Cornish Riviera Express* past 6877 *Llanfair Grange* in the yard, 5 July 1956. (GW Trust)

1016 *County* of Hants starts out of Ruabon with a stopping train from Chester to Shrewsbury, 9 August 1956. (GW Trust)

1000 *County* of Middlesex in BR passenger green livery at Bristol Temple Meads after arriving with a local train from Swindon, c1957. (MLS Collection)

1019 *County of Merioneth* running in after major overhaul at Swindon and repainting in lined Brunswick green livery, on an empty 'B' set leaving Bristol Temple Meads eastbound, 6 July 1957.
(GW Trust)

Neyland's 1020 *County of Monmouth* in the Peterston area between Bridgend and Cardiff with the 8.48am Fishguard – Paddington parcels train, 23 November 1957.
(J. Hodge)

Bath Road's 1028 *County of Warwick* speeds through Chipping Sodbury with the 11.45am Bristol-Paddington express, c1957.
(GW Trust)

The highest speed I have seen recorded by a 'County' (reported in the August 1956 edition of *Trains Illustrated*) was surprisingly on the descent into Shrewsbury, down the final 1 in 100 to Coton Hill, when 1017 *County of Hereford* was timed at 83½mph. It had run the 17.2 miles from Gobowen in 17 minutes 9 seconds, although with only a load of seven coaches, 246/270 tons. Inevitably the train was then checked by signals and the section to the Shrewsbury stop was completed in three seconds under twenty minutes. 1017 was still with single chimney at the time.

After the two-year trials with the draughting of 1009 in an attempt to improve the always suspect steaming of the 'County' boiler, the equipping of the fleet with the new standard double-chimney design began in May 1956, and I have come across some logs from the Railway Performance Society's archives of 'County' runs in the Midlands at about this time.

A couple were timed between Banbury and Birmingham, one with a single and one with a double-chimney and from first sight perversely the single-chimney engine seemed the better although with a two-coach lighter train. The double-chimney engine was faster away but the single chimney engine (on a tighter schedule) was driven harder downhill. Taking the Leamington stop and heavier train into account, honours were even on Hatton Bank.

Banbury-Birmingham Snow Hill

		10.10am Paddington-Aberystwyth, 23.2.57			9.20am Bournemouth-Birkenhead, 13.4.57		
		1017 *County of Hereford* (Single chimney)			1022 *County of Northampton* (Double chimney)		
		8 chs, 278/295 tons			10 chs, 342/360 tons		
Distance Miles	Location	Times mins secs	Speed mph		Times mins secs	Speed mph	
0.0	Banbury	00.00		2 L	00.00		5 L
1.7	Ironstone Sdgs	03.44	41		03.34	41	
3.6	Cropredy	06.18	48		06.06	50	
5.05	MP 91 ¼	08.03	47		07.47	49	
6.8	MP 93	10.02	56		09.52	53	
8.8	Fenny Compton	11.55	67		11.58	61	
11.8	MP 98	14.28	74		14.45	69	
13.75	Southam Road	16.09	64		16.29	61	
16.2	Fosse Road	18.15	75		18.50	64	
19.9	Leamington	22.19	sigs 30*		22.57 / 00.00		
21.8	Warwick	24.40	56/54		03.29	45/42	
26.0	Hatton	29.38	51/44		09.37	46/35	
30.2	Lapworth	34.27	pws 43*/60/56		-	58/ pws 15*	
32.7	Knowle	37.10	55		20.23	38	
36.1	Solihull	40.27	66/64		24.41	51	
39.9	Tyseley	43.43	72/70		28.47	60	
43.2	Birmingham	47.46		1 E	32.47		5 L

A further run from Leamington to Wolverhampton with the newly double-chimneyed 1022.

8.56am Ramsgate-Birkenhead (nicknamed 'The Conti')
1022 *County of Northampton*
12 chs 403/425 tons

Distance Miles	Location	Times mins secs	Speed mph		
0.0	Leamington	00.00		10 L	
1.9	Warwick	04.03	43		
6.1	Hatton	10.35	44/32/37 ½	10¾ L	
10.3	Lapworth	15.25	60/58		
12.9	Knowle	18.04	57/62		
16.2	Solihull	21.24	65/71		
20.0	Tyseley	24.35	73½	10¾ L	
23.3	Birmingham	28.10	(fast in)	8¼ L	
0.0		00.00		8¾ L	
	Handsworth Jn	06.50	38/34	9¼ L	1 in 100R
	Swan Village	10.02	50		
7.4	Wednesbury	12.10	38*/50		
10.9	Priestfield	16.45	39*		
12.6	Wolverhampton	19.49		8¾ L	

1007 *County* of *Brecknock*, newly overhauled and equipped with new style double chimney, running in on a Swindon – Bristol local train, emerges from Twerton Tunnel near Bath, May 1957 (J.M. Bentley Collection)

Although the 'Counties' seemed most suited to Devon and Cornwall, the North & West and the route north of Wolverhampton, where the drivers could exploit their capacity for short bursts of power, the Bristol fleet of engines seemed still to work turn and turn about with Bath Road 'Castles' except on the fastest turns like the *Bristolian* (although 'Modified Halls' have worked that train in an emergency, there is no record of a 'County' having done so). O.S. Nock was a frequent traveller in the 1950s between Bath and London and recorded a number of journeys. On the very fast 1.15pm Paddington-Bristol, allowed 96½ minutes in the summer 1954 timetable for the 106.9 miles to first stop Bath, normally reserved for a 'Castle', 1000 *County of Middlesex* achieved a net time of 94½ minutes with the booked seven-coach 252 ton train, averaging 71.3mph between Southall and Twyford after a fast departure from Paddington, 70.1mph average Pangbourne to Steventon, and 69.7mph Steventon-Shrivenham. Top speed was 76½mph at Dauntsey where a 'Castle' would normally be doing 85mph on this train and the actual time to Bath was 101 minutes, 4½ minutes late, caused by a 30mph check through Reading and a p-way

slack to 15 mph just before Swindon at Marston. Nock's comment was, 'Not bad, but could have done better.'

With a much heavier load (12 coaches, 403/440 tons) on the 6.30pm Paddington-Plymouth via Bristol, 1009 *County of Carmarthen* in September 1960 ran the 94 miles to the first stop, Chippenham, in 103 minutes 39 seconds (92 minutes net) with 71mph at Slough before a p-way slack just after Maidenhead, 66mph through Didcot, signal checks before Swindon and 78mph down Dauntsey Bank. I suggest that these runs are not exceptional, but fairly typical of normal 'County' performance on level track.

1009, *County of Carmarthen,* the locomotive which was the guinea-pig for the new style double chimney in 1954, here equipped with the evolved design, leaving Newton Abbot with a Plymouth-Exeter train, 2 July 1957. (GW Trust)

Truro's 1023 *County of Oxford* at Truro with the Penzance portion of a London train, July 1957. (J.M. Bentley Collection/ Photomatic)

1011 *County* of *Chester* assists 6016 *King Edward V* on the climb past Stoneycombe to Dainton summit with a Paddington-Penzance express, 3 July 1957. (GW Trust)

Shrewsbury's top link 1016 *County of Hants* is entrusted with the Salop/ Newton Abbot shared double-home diagram, normally a 'Castle' turn, the 8am Plymouth-Crewe/Liverpool, between Teignmouth and Dawlish, 31 July 1957. (GW Trust)

1009 *County* of *Carmarthen* climbs through Ponthir between Newport and Pontypool Road with the 10.05am Penzance-Liverpool, after changing engines and departing Bristol at 2.30pm, 20 June 1957. (J. Hodge)

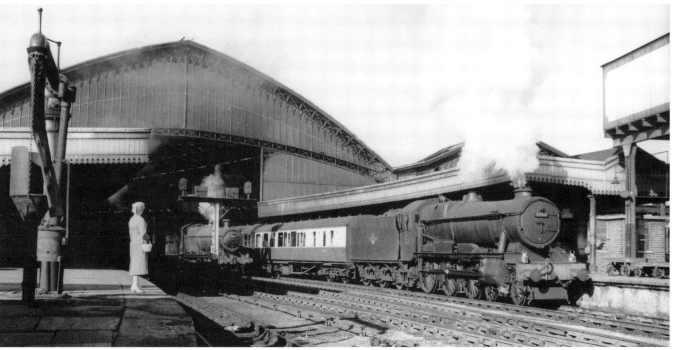

1000 *County* of *Middlesex*, its large double chimney replaced with the standard squat version, departs Bristol with the 11.45am to Paddington past a Churchward 28XX standing with a freight on the centre road, c1957. (J.M. Bentley Collection/ G. Heiron)

1002 *County* of *Berks* crosses the viaduct into Truro station with the down *Cornish Riviera Express*, 15 June 1958.
(GW Trust)

1016 *County* of *Hants* with the 10.35am Penzance *Cornishman* near Plymouth, 15 July 1958.
(R.C. Riley)

1010 *County* of *Caernarvon* piloting 7909 *Heveningham Hall* on the 2pm Penzance-Crewe at Largin, 1 July 1958.
(Colour Rail/T. Owen)

1006 *County* of *Cornwall*, still in black livery and with single chimney, hauling a holiday express on St Pinnock Viaduct in Cornwall, 1 September 1958.
(R.C. Riley)

1002 *County* of *Berks* at Cowley Bridge Junction, Exeter, with a down parcels train, 14 May 1959.
(MLS Collection)

1011 *County* of *Chester* assists an unidentified 'Hall' on a heavy 13-coach Penzance-Paddington holiday train passing Powderham, near Exeter, summer 1959.
(MLS Collection/J. Davenport)

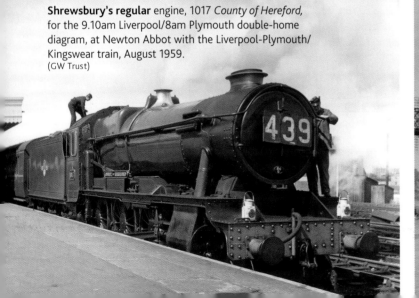

Shrewsbury's regular engine, 1017 *County of Hereford,* for the 9.10am Liverpool/8am Plymouth double-home diagram, at Newton Abbot with the Liverpool-Plymouth/Kingswear train, August 1959.
(GW Trust)

Another of Shrewsbury's 'Counties' in excellent condition, 1016 *County of Hants* on a West of England-Liverpool express passing Norton Fitzwarren, 8 August1959.
(MLS Collection)

1023 *County* of *Oxford* with the 1.30pm Paddington *Royal Duchy* near Truro, 21 September 1959.
(GW Trust)

1015 *County* of *Gloucester* at Exeter St David's with a NE/SW express, 13 April 1959.
(GW Trust)

1014 *County of Glamorgan* at Twyford with the 7.5am Cheltenham-Paddington, 31 May 1958 .
(Colour Rail/T. Owen)

1015 *County of Gloucester* is unusual power for the 3.30pm Paddington-Plymouth in May 1958, seen here in Sonning Cutting. This fast Plymouth service was normally a 'King' turn or 'Castle' if a 'King' was not available. 1015 is still in single-chimney form, not receiving its double-chimney and repaint until November 1958.
(Colour Rail/T. Owen)

1024 *County* of
Pembroke near
Kingskerswell with a
Paignton/Manchester
train, 1959.
(Les Folkard/Online Transport
Trust)

1018 *County* of
Leicester on the 10.45am
Penzance-Sheffield meets
6959 *Peatling Hall* on
the 7.43am Nottingham-
Plymouth at the entrance
to Parson's Rock Tunnel,
Dawlish, 20 August 1960.
(MLS Collection/O.H.S. Owen)

By the late 1950s, dieselisation with the 'Warship' hydraulics had displaced the 'Counties' from the West Country and their numbers were strengthened in West Wales, working from Neyland depot on milk trains, freight and an occasional stopping passenger train. The only log I can find of a Neyland 'County' was of 1029 *County of Worcester* on 28 August 1956, when it hauled a thirteen-coach London express from Swansea as far as Cardiff, in a running time of 73 minutes with stops at Neath, Port Talbot and Bridgend. No speeds were recorded apart from a maximum of 60mph near Llantrisant. In the 1960s, they could be found still operating from Bristol St Philips Marsh to South Wales, Swindon, Pontypool Road and Shrewsbury, although their London work was dieselised by then. Their last workings were Shrewsbury engines north of Wolverhampton on the Chester portions of London trains until replaced by LM 'Black 5s' after the Regional boundary change, and on the North and West in the Spring of 1963 following diesel shortages after the severe 1962/3 winter. A number also finished at Swindon undertaking fairly humdrum parcels, freight and stopping passenger duties with an occasional rail enthusiast special thrown in. The last survivors were 1000 at St Philips Marsh, 1010 and 1013 at Swindon, all three withdrawn in July 1964 and 1011 *County of Chester* which departed in November 1964 after a number of enthusiast 'last rite' specials, including a Stephenson Locomotive Society special on 20 September.

1007 *County* of *Brecknock* near Swan Village with the first up Wolverhampton-Paddington service, 2 August 1960. (MLS Collection)

1022 *County of Northampton* departs Paddington past Subway Junction with the 1.50pm Relief Paddington-Carmarthen , 10 September 1960.
(R.C. Riley)

1004 *County of Somerset* with the 8.55am Birkenhead-Paddington parcels, a notorious late-runner at this time, passing Wednesbury, 28 May 1960.
(R.C. Riley)

1027 *County* of *Stafford* and another GW 4-6-0 wait to cross to Ranelagh Bridge, Paddington to turn before returning to their home depots, 27.8.1960. Both firemen are pulling coal forward ready for their return working. (R.C. Riley)

1012 *County* of *Denbigh* heads westwards with a Plymouth-Truro stopping train, shortly after leaving the city of Plymouth, c1960. (GW trust)

1019 *County* of *Merioneth* at Taunton with a Taunton-Exeter stopping train, c1961. (GW Trust)

1003 *County of Wilts* passing Iver on the Down Relief Line with a fitted freight from Paddington Goods, 9 March 1961. (Colour Rail)

1024 *County* of *Pembroke* passing Highbridge with a West of England-Manchester express, 22 May 1961. Z13 would be a special train of some sort, but the stock looks like that of a booked service, so the smokebox door chalked inscription probably belongs to a previous working. 1024 does not look as though it has seen the attentions of a cleaner for several days. (MLS Collection)

1010 *County of Caernarvon* climbing Dainton bank with the 8.50am Bradford-Plymouth, c1961.
(GW Trust/C. Owen)

1000 *County of Middlesex* passes Southall with the 3pm Kensington-Laira milk empties, c1961.
(GW Trust)

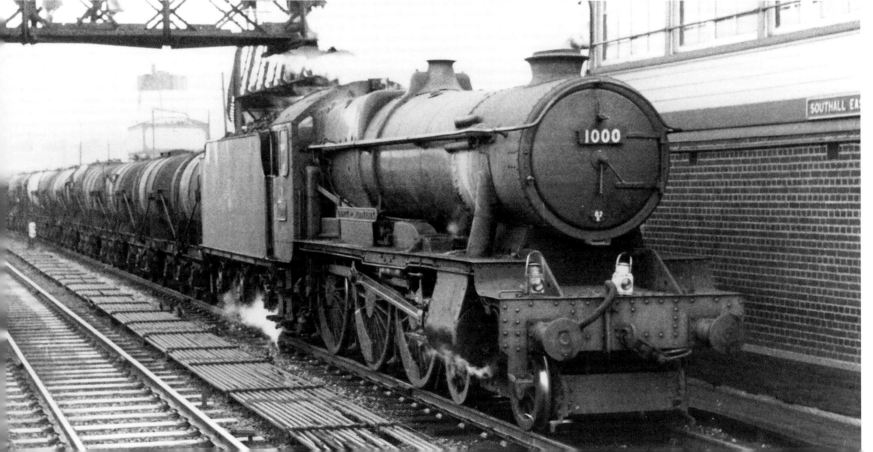

1025 *County of Radnor* passing Chester Racecourse with the 3.50pm Birkenhead-Paddington which it will work to Wolverhampton where a 'King' will attach the restaurant car portion for the run to London, 21 April 1960.
(MLS Collection)

1013 *County* of *Dorset* at Leamington with a down fitted freight, c1961.
(GW Trust)

1022 *County* of
Northampton enters
Newport station with the
5.10pm Cardiff-Pontypool
Road-N & W semi-fast
service, 1961.
(J. Hodge)

Shrewsbury's 1025
County of Radnor with
a return Barry Island-
Tyseley excursion train,
6 August 1961.
(J. Hodge)

1009 *County of Carmarthen* enters Tiverton Junction station with the 4.30pm Taunton-Exeter stopping train, 15 June 1962. (R.C. Riley)

1024 *County of Pembroke* comes off the Berks & Hants at Reading with an up parcels train, c1962. Note the gaggle of small boy trainspotters on the far platform, still a common sight in the early 1960s. (GW Trust)

Neyland's 1027 *County of Stafford* at Whitland with the 2.40pm Neyland-Paddington which it will work only as far as Carmarthen, 6 September 1962. Neyland had so little work for its large engines that its cleaners seem to have had the opportunity to keep their 'Counties' looking smart until the end, unlike most other 'County' depots.
(MLS Collection/W.A. Brown)

1008 *County* of Cardigan on the Chester and Birkenhead portion of a train from Paddington, near Baschurch, 4 November 1962.
(MLS Collection/N.K. Harrop)

1001 *County* of *Bucks* with a West Wales stopping passenger train at Clarbeston Road opposite an unidentified 'Hall', c1963.
(J.M. Bentley Collection)

The end is nigh! 1001 *County of Bucks* leaves Neyland with the 2.40pm express to Paddington, which it will haul to Carmarthen only, past a stored pannier tank, c1963. 1001 was withdrawn in June 1963.
(J.M. Bentley Collection)

1000 *County* of *Middlesex* departs from Gloucester with a fitted freight, c Spring 1964. (GW Trust)

1011 *County* of *Chester* arrives at Weymouth with a light semi-fast train from Bristol and Westbury, 10 May 1964. (GW Trust)

1010 *County* of *Caernarvon* near Southall with the Kensington-Laira milk empties, shortly before its withdrawal in July 1964.
(GW Trust)

1011 *County* of *Chester* being prepared at Swindon for the 'farewell' tour X83 in the Swindon-Birmingham-Gloucester-Swindon round trip run by the Stephenson Locomotive Society (SLS), 20 September 1964.
(GW Trust)

1011 *County* of *Chester* climbs Sapperton Bank on its final return to Swindon with the SLS special train, 20 September 1964. (GW Trust)

1014 *County* of *Glamorgan* trailing its empty stock out of Paddington back to Old Oak Common after arriving with a train from Bristol, April 1953. (David Maidment)

Personal Experience

My first encounter with a 'County' was not, surprisingly, during a holiday in Paignton in 1952, when days of trainspotting from the beach at both Goodrington and Teignmouth produced a 'nil' return. My 'first' sighting instead was during a regular day out as a 14-year-old round the London termini in April 1953, when I photographed 1014 *County of Glamorgan* resplendent in BR mixed traffic black and LNWR lining livery backing out of Paddington station after earlier arrival with an express from Bristol. After that, I gradually accumulated numbers through my excursions to London and travels elsewhere, but I took no more photos of any of them until I captured 1019 *County of Merioneth* on a parcels (somewhat unsuccessfully) at Oxford in March 1956 as I was attempting (equally unsuccessfully) to get a scholarship to the university.

During an eight month 'gap year' work experience as a relief clerk at Old Oak Common in 1957, most of it spent as the 'engine history clerk' in the Mechanical Foreman's office, I remember little of 'Counties'. This indicates that they were rare visitors, as I would tour the shed daily (my clerical work was not very onerous) noting engines of interest and I can recollect no 'Counties' in my vivid memories of the period. However, towards the end of my time there, I was eligible for my first rail 'free pass' and went down to Swansea overnight on the fast newspaper train, returning on the *Swansea Pullman* next day – both with 'Castles' (5084 & 5077). After early morning visits to Swansea Docks and Danygraig depots, I had a shed permit to Landore and when I was ready to walk back to High Street station, I was hailed by a driver from the cab of Neyland's 1001 *County of Bucks* and offered a footplate 'hitch' back to the station, which of course I quickly accepted. 1001 was in superb condition, but

was dropping down to the station for a westbound parcels train.

My 1958 summer sojourn at Old Oak during the university vacation produced no memories

of 'Counties' either, but I bought a weekly season ticket from Paddington to Reading (cost 15/-) in June 1959 to sample some of the engines and crews I knew

Neyland's 1001 *County of Bucks* on which the author was offered a footplate 'lift' from Landore shed back to Swansea High Street station, before it was coupled to a parcel train for West Wales, August 1957.
(David Maidment)

1019 *County of Merioneth* running in after overhaul and equipping with a 4-row superheater boiler, on a Swindon-Reading local train after arrival at Reading, just three months before the run described, 25 March 1959. 1019 was one of the last 'Counties' to exchange its single chimney for the new pattern double blastpipe and chimney.
(GW Trust)

on the road. I spent six days see-sawing to and fro, with three or four return journeys a day before repairing back home to Woking. In that week, I travelled behind just two 'Counties', an extreme experience of good and bad. 1019 *County of Merioneth*, by then a double-chimney engine based at Swindon, ran into Reading from Gloucester on 17 June on the train due Paddington at 10.30am. It had eight coaches, 264/290 tons and roared out of Reading, making the fastest start of the week in the up direction, passing Twyford, 5.0 miles, in 6 minutes 48 seconds already travelling at 68mph. A maximum of 77mph saw us through Maidenhead in 12 minutes, 35 seconds and Slough in under even time, 17.5 miles in 17 minutes 14 seconds. We slowed slightly for Slough (73mph) then accelerated again to 79mph – my highest with a 'County' – before a p-way slowing to 15mph at Hayes. 68mph at Ealing Broadway, then signal checks all the way into the terminus made us take 42½ minutes overall, arriving 2 minutes late, but our net time was the even 36 minutes.

1012 *County* of *Denbigh* waiting attention at Swindon Works, c1960. (GW Trust)

On the Saturday, 20th, I was surprised to find Swindon's 1012 *County of Denbigh* in place of the booked Cardiff 'Britannia' on the 1.55pm Paddington which stopped at Reading on Saturdays. I gathered from conversation with the crew that it was a hastily prepared replacement for a failed pacific, and the subsequent run was dire. A signal check to 10mph at Acton did not help and we struggled to reach 50mph before the Hayes bridge slack to 15mph. It just got worse after that. The twelve-coach train seemed too much for the locomotive which was clearly struggling for steam and we took 49¼ minutes to get to Reading without exceeding 56 mph anywhere.

The following year, after college final examinations, I celebrated by purchasing another Paddington-Reading weekly season for the six days commencing 20 June 1960. My very first trip of the week found me choosing between a 'Castle' on the heavy 8.55am Paddington-West Wales and the eleven-coach 405ton gross 9.5am to Weston-super-Mare which had Penzance 1008 *County of Cardigan* at the head. I chose the 'rare' 'County' and had a mediocre 42 minute net run to Reading with a 25mph signal check at Old Oak Common and a dead stand for half a minute at milepost 26 just west of Maidenhead lengthening the actual time to 49 minutes. Speed in between steadied between 60 and 64mph from Hayes to Maidenhead and never really recovered from the MP26 check. Later in the week, I had a couple of brighter 'County' runs. 1028 *County of Warwick* ran up well enough with an evening arrival from Bristol, but after timing

1008 *County* of Cardigan, a Penzance engine, at Saltash with a Penzance-Plymouth train, c1960.
(GW Trust)

1028 *County* of Warwick at Bristol Bath Road, its home depot, with a Hall, 4575 class 2-6-2T and a pannier tank, 12 April 1959.
(MLS Collection)

Bristol Bath Road's 1009 *County of Carmarthen* on Canton shed alongside a WD 2-8-0 and BR Standard '4' 75022, 18 April 1956.
(J. Hodge)

all day, I was weary and rested my eyes. I did time 1009 *County of Carmarthen* on the up *Merchant Venturer* on the Saturday evening. The train was a heavy twelve-coach 435 ton gross load, and it ran into Reading nearly five minutes late.

1009 accelerated hard and passed Twyford in 7 minutes 6 seconds at 64mph. The engine then continued to accelerate the train and steadied at 72-74mph until eased after Iver, having passed Slough in 18 minutes 41 seconds. It was then opened

up again and ran from Southall to Acton at a sustained 72-73 mph before a slight signal check at Westbourne Park. The actual overall time was 39 minutes 10 seconds (38 net) and arrival was two minutes late.

Later that year, after joining the Western Region in August as a permanent employee, I began to use my 'privilege tickets' for evening jaunts after work. I caught the 6.5pm Paddington-Oxford commuter train one evening when I saw a Shrewsbury 'County' backing on (1026 *County of Salop*) instead of the usual Oxford 'Castle', but regretted I had the usual lacklustre run that I was beginning to get on alternate runs with the class. Suffice to say we took 49 minutes to get to Reading ('Counties' seemed stuck on that figure) which included a one minute stop at Hayes. We did wake up a little after that check (the driver braking too hard for the Hayes bridge slowing?) and got our thirteen-coach train packed with home-going commuters up to 68mph at Taplow. I had a run behind Oxford's double-chimney 'Castle', 5033, a couple of months later and that did even worse, taking 44 minutes unchecked without exceeding 65mph.

During a series of visits to the North and West in February 1961, I took a photo of 1025 County of Radnor at Shrewsbury and my next experience of the class was in October after I had become a Western Region 'Traffic Apprentice' (management trainee) and was undertaking my initial station training at Maidenhead, based at lodgings in Reading. I commuted most days from Reading on the 6.45am Swindon which was actually rostered for one of the three Didcot 'Counties' (1002, 1015, 1018) but was often a 'Modified Hall' or any engine that Swindon found on hand that included that month an Old Oak Common 47XX 2-8-0 and a St Philips Marsh Churchward mogul. I timed

1026 *County* of Salop allocated to Shrewsbury and seen here at its home depot, 8 November 1958.
(J. Hodge)

1025 **County** of Radnor on a late evening two-coach local train to Wellington, with a Collett 0-6-0 32XX goods engine in the bay alongside.
(David Maidment)

the twelve mile run most days and absolutely typically had the best and worst runs on successive days behind the same 'County' – 1018

County of Leicester. The train was normally nine coaches, 306/340 tons and was scheduled fifteen minutes start-to-stop. The 'County' runs I

timed are tabled below, showing the Twyford passing time from Reading and the time when the train was at a stand at Maidenhead.

Date:	26.9.61		6.10.61		7.11.61		8.11.61		9.11.61		10.11.61	
Loco:	1015		1015		1018		1018		1018		1018	
Reading	00.00		00.00		00.00		00.00		00.00		00.00	
Twyford	07.25	60	08.00	61	07.25	61	07.03	64	08.45	51	07.17	62
Waltham	12.31	64	12.46	69	12.13	68	11.34	68	14.23	55	12.04	66
Maidenhead	15.05		15.12		14.47		13.57		17.45		14.32	

I did not time the train every day, as sometimes I was travelling with a colleague or the train was too crowded to time properly. I had one run with 1002, the other Didcot 'County' which I failed to time. I did time seven runs with 'Halls', two 'Granges', and one each with 4701 and 6364. The only engine to touch 70mph at Waltham Sidings was the 5ft 8in 'Grange', 6851 of Oxley. The fastest start to Twyford was Didcot 'Hall' 4994 although 1018 on 8th had just overtaken it by

Ruscombe. 4701 took 15½ minutes, top speed 63mph and the St Philips Marsh 2-6-0, 16½ minutes, just touching 60mph. The following month I was training at Slough Goods depot and took the 7.30am Oxford-Paddington, non-stop from Reading to the Slough stop. This train also had nine coaches and was always hauled by one of Oxford's 'Castles'. It is therefore interesting to compare the Reading-Waltham time of the 'Castles' with the 'Counties'. Twelve runs

with 5012, 5025 and 5033 averaged 12 minutes 10 seconds, exactly 30 seconds faster than the 'County' average. On most days, they were half a minute slower to Twyford, but then usually topped 70mph before Maidenhead with 74mph the highest with 5012 on two occasions, both runs beating 1018's fastest time to Waltham Sidings. In the evening, I usually travelled back from Maidenhead on the 4.35pm Paddington-Swindon that would have any Bristol Division engine that Old Oak happened to have on hand including a Penzance Grange (6808) and an ex-works 4079 *Pendennis Castle*. One 'County', 1000 itself, appeared on this train in November 1961.

Armed with quarter-fare 'privilege tickets' I frequently travelled out to Swindon or Banbury of an evening and on Saturdays would go further afield. A favourite was to go down to Bristol on the 7.30am Paddington-Plymouth until it was dieselised, pick up the 8am Plymouth-Liverpool 83A/84G double-home turn and come home on the 4.30pm Birkenhead from Shrewsbury. On 18 November, I went down on a 'Warship' hauled *Bristolian*, and got Shrewsbury's excellent 5038 on the punctual Plymouth-Liverpool. The 4.30pm Birkenhead

One of the three Didcot 'Counties' allocated for commuter and parcels train duties in 1961-2. 1002 *County of Berks* hustles a morning commuter train from Didcot and Reading through Langley on the up relief line, 23 April 1962. (J.M. Bentley Collection)

changed engines at Shrewsbury and again at Wolverhampton, with a Shrewsbury 'Castle', 'County' or 'Hall' being diagrammed for the Salop-Wolverhampton leg. On this day I was lucky, I thought, to get Shrewsbury's double-chimney 1022 *County of Northampton* on the twelve-coach restaurant car express, 425 tons gross. Unfortunately, it seemed to be my day for the alternate 'County' poor performance. Although 1022 looked good and made plenty of noise, it seemed to be getting

nowhere, only managing 35mph on the 1 in 120 before Wellington. The next leg was worse taking over ten minutes to clear the four mile 1 in 132/220 to Hollinswood at 29mph, and dropping from 62 to 36mph from Cosford to the summit beyond Albrighton handing over five minutes late to 'Castle' 7017 at Wolverhampton.

At the end of April 1962, I was assigned to Old Oak Common for three months motive power training including footplate work. I was

required to undertake a variety of duties, steam and diesel, including a steam-hauled stopping passenger service – somewhat difficult to find in the London Division in 1962. However, on a Saturday some DMU turns became engine and coaches, and I joined the SO 12noon Paddington-Oxford, first stop Reading, then all stations. I had my baptism of driving with 'Hall' 5986 to Didcot, then to my surprise exchanged the 'Hall' for Didcot's 1015 *County of Gloucester* for the

Didcot's 1002 *County of Berks* in a typically filthy condition, seen here at Didcot, 1962.
(GW Trust)

short run onto Oxford. The engine was not exerted of course on an all stations train of eight non-corridor coaches. I mainly remember the spaciousness of the 'County' cab after the other GW engines I had already ridden on. I was very conscious of the fore-and-aft movement, as I was standing on the footplate of the Hawksworth flush-sided tender. I had planned to return to London on the very fast 5.30pm Oxford-Paddington allowed exactly the hour for the 63 miles with just six coaches. On weekdays, it was booked for a top-link Old Oak 'Castle' but on Saturdays it

was diagrammed for an Oxford engine and I was told that the depot often borrowed one of the Didcot 'Counties' for the job. In fact, I had guessed (wrongly) that the reason for the engine change at Didcot was to get 1015 to Oxford for the turn. However, I got an Oxford 'Modified Hall' (7911) which reached London in 59 minutes with running in the low eighties for much of the way. Despite what I was told, I have never seen the log of a 'County' on this train – it would have been very interesting to see how a 'County' coped with continuous high speed for an hour's duration.

Later, on 17 May, I had gone down to Shrewsbury on the footplate of a 'King' (which I had fired) then a 'Castle' and I had intended to return in the cab of the engines working the 4.30pm Birkenhead. I was shattered, however, after my down line exertions, and I regret to say that I rejected the opportunity of riding on the footplate of 1026 *County of Salop,* in whose running I took little interest as I cleaned myself up sufficiently to appear on the cushions among ordinary passengers.

At the end of August 1962. just completing my marshalling yard training at Margam, I took a Saturday off to experience 'Kings' on the Wolverhampton line before the class 52s (D10XX) took over at the beginning of the winter timetable. I missed 6007 on the 10.10 *Cambrian Coast Express* as the ticket queue at Paddington was too long, the 11.10 had a class 52 'Western' hydraulic, so I settled for the 12.10 with 6019. 5047 took this to Shrewsbury where I waited for the 1.10pm Paddington whose Chester portion turned up behind another Stafford Road 'Castle', 5031, which I joined to Gobowen before needing to alight to catch the last up London, the 4.30pm Birkenhead. This ran in with Shrewsbury's 1017 *County of Hereford* with eight coaches, 277/305 tons. This was my turn for a good 'County' run, so we roared out of Gobowen down the 1 in 156, accelerating to 66mph inside three minutes, touched 73 in the dip before Rednal, fell back to 68 up the short 1 in 136, then up to 74 again on the undulating railway before the rise to Baschurch, where we braked to 63mph before 72 again and the falling gradients

Didcot's 1015 *County of Gloucester* photographed here at Oxford shed in 1962, about the time that the author footplated it between Didcot and Oxford on the Saturday stopping train from Paddington. (J. Hodge)

through Leaton. The eighteen miles were covered in 19 minutes 46 seconds and the 10 minute late start had been reduced to 7¾ minutes. Shrewsbury effected the engine change to double-chimney 'Castle' 7015 five minutes under schedule and the 'Castle' drew into Wolverhampton a minute early. Reading's 5018 (on loan to Wolverhampton) then romped away and arrived at Paddington station eleven minutes early, an experience I was not used to on this train. In fact, all six locomotives I had sampled that day performed excellently – a last fling with steam before the diesels came south of Wolverhampton.

True to form the next 'County' experience was below par. I should have guessed as much when, on 1 September 1962, 1003 *County of Wilts* of Laira crept into Bristol Temple Meads 23 minutes late on the 6.10am Penzance-Manchester instead of the booked 'Warship' hydraulic. However, I was delighted and joined the twelve-coach 408/445 ton train. The start was inauspicious as we crawled from signal to signal departing from Temple Meads as far as Ashley Hill, then opened up to a painful 17mph, at least overtaking 1M14 with 4914 *Cranmore Hall* which was stuck, waiting for us, on the relief line. We freewheeled down to the Severn Tunnel at 76mph before signals again nearly brought us to a stand, took six and a half minutes to clear the tunnel itself with 26mph at Severn Tunnel West. Running in the low 40s along the level to Maindee Junction was pitiful, but we did display some energy climbing through Llantarnam Junction up the long 1 in 106/95 to Pontypool

1026 *County* of *Salop* at Saltney Junction with the Birkenhead-Wolverhampton portion of an express destined for Paddington, 19 February 1962 – a footplate experience the author regrettably turned down three months later.
(MLS Collection/W.A. Brown)

1017 *County* of Hereford, a regular performer from Shrewsbury shed on the Wolverhampton-Chester services at the end of WR steam, 28 November 1959.
(J. Hodge)

Road at a respectable 31mph. I suspect the driver was nursing the engine after Severn Tunnel Junction whilst the fireman worked on the fire to tackle the gradients ahead. However, after Pontypool Road performance deteriorated again. We started the climb to Llanvihangel at 58mph and fell to 24½ at the summit. It could have been a lot worse; at least we did not stop for a banker with this heavy load. We drifted downhill, blower hard on, in the mid-fifties and finally eased into Hereford station in 48 minutes exactly from Pontypool Road, now 25½ late. I suppose, in view of the checks, this was not too bad, but it was a very easy Saturday schedule. The 'County' was clearly in trouble for steam, so I alighted and decided to try the next service, 1M14 I'd seen earlier. This was a revelation. With ten coaches, we soon caught up 1003 – a minute stop just after

Leominster, more checks before Ludlow and Onibury and then miraculously we got a clear road to Marshbrook, so 1003 must have been having one of its mini-spurts. The 'Hall was sustaining 51mph on the climb before the 25mph check, then recovered to 36mph at Church Stretton and ran up to an unusual 75mph at Dorrington and a clear road into Shrewsbury with no sign of 1003 or its train. If 1003 would not go uphill, it had clearly been driven hard down.

During the heavy snowfalls of January 1963, I was at Plymouth undertaking some training at Laira diesel depot, and each morning found a row of steam locomotives queued under the coaling stage. By this time, Plymouth was meant to be steam-free but the snows had taken their toll of the diesels and some of Laira's stored engines came out to the rescue including

'Castles' 4087 and 7022. However, it was too late for Laira's 'Counties' as there was a row of withdrawn engines including several of them, headed by the now nameless 1015. I travelled home to Woking each weekend, with potential steam if I could get it as far as Exeter St David's where I transferred to the Southern. One Friday, I managed 6990 on a single-engine load, but on 8 February I found 1021 *County of Montgomery* of St Philips Marsh was the train engine for the 4pm mail and passenger train to Crewe and Glasgow, provided with D1008 *Western Harrier* as pilot to Newton Abbot. The load including the Royal Mail van was nine vehicles, 335 tons gross. We were badly delayed at the start and came to a dead stand at Tavistock Junction for half a minute and could only accelerate to 50mph by Plympton when we encountered the 1 in 42 of Hemerdon Bank. Both locomotives were now working flat out – the noise from both grew to a crescendo echoing from the tree-lined banks – and after falling to 31mph, the 'County' was opened out even more and the two engines surmounted the fearsome bank at 34mph. Then it was plain sailing on the steam engine and the 'County' only woke up again after a p-way restriction to 15mph through Totnes station, so the pair had to do a repeat performance on Dainton, accelerating initially to 53mph on the 1 in 105, then falling back to 36mph as they hit the steepest section of 1 in 37/43. Speed downhill had, however, been very restrained, never exceeding 55mph, and the initial delays plus the p-way slack caused us to be two minutes late into Exeter.

1003 *County of Wilts* at Banbury on a Wolverhampton-Bournemouth cross-country train made up with Southern rolling stock, 1962.
(J.M. Bentley Collection)

The following Monday morning, returning to resume training in South Wales, I chose to travel as far as Reading on the 11.15 Paddington-Worcester train with steam, changing there to the 11.55 Cardiff train with a Hymek. It was unexpected to get a Bristol based 'County' on this train and I was heartened by a vigorous departure from Paddington passing Southall in a few seconds under thirteen minutes at 63mph. 1028 *County of Warwick* continued energetically with its nine coach train passing Slough half a minute early at 72mph. The driver then eased the engine and we settled down to a steady 68-70mph until Sonning Cutting. The driver had taken this a little too easily as the timing of this train was quite sharp – 38 minutes for the 36 miles – and we stopped in 38 minutes 31 seconds from London.

For the next three months, I was training in the South Wales Divisional office in Cardiff based at Marland House opposite Cardiff General station, and most mornings a colleague Traffic Apprentice and I would commute to Newport and back on the 8.20am Cardiff-Manchester which was regularly hauled by a Pontypool Road 'Hall' or 'Grange' until it joined the Bristol portion there with its Brush Type 4 diesel. If we were expected in the office by 9 o'clock we would have to return on a Bristol-Cardiff cross-country DMU, but if it was not so urgent we would wait for a steam semi-fast off the Shrewsbury line with either one of the Salop based 'Jubilees' or a 'County' or Hereford-based 'Hall'. I noted 1005,

1015 *County of Gloucester* standing, after withdrawal, among a row of withdrawn engines including another couple of 'Counties' at Laira depot during the harsh winter of 1963. (David Maidment)

1021 *County of Montgomery* on the 4pm Plymouth-Crewe Royal Mail train during the 1962/3 winter when many diesel turns were replaced by steam following failures in the icy conditions. 1021 would work the train to Bristol Temple Meads, piloted by class 52, D1008 *Western Harrier*, over the South Devon banks to Newton Abbot, 8 February 1963. (David Maidment)

1006 (on consecutive days), 1011 (four times) and 1020 on this turn, though we did not time what was usually a humdrum trot between Newport and Cardiff without any real excitement. We did touch a very rare 79mph one day – some 20mph faster than usual – but that was with an ex-works 'Hall', not a 'County'.

In the Spring of 1963, temporary reversion to steam traction occurred between Bristol and Shrewsbury for two through expresses in each direction. The diesel substitute power was a St Philips Marsh 'Castle' or 'County'

and my Traffic Apprentice colleague and I had frequent trips through April and May picking up either the 2pm or 4pm from Plymouth at Pontypool Road and going to Hereford or a couple of times right through to Shrewsbury. Extra power was transferred to St Philips Marsh for the work, and two transferred double-chimney 'Castles', 4087 and 4093, seemed the pick of the bunch and could be relied on for excellent performances on the diesel schedules. I decided one day to go to Bristol and travel on the 2pm Plymouth right through to

Shrewsbury. The date was 5 April 1963 and instead of the expected 'Castle', 1021 *County of Montgomery* replaced the Laira 'Warship'. The load was 4 coaches and four parcel vans from Bristol with an extra coach added on the front at Pontypool Road turning a three minute early arrival into a three minute late departure. The run was curiously uneven with bursts of energy followed by easings – typical of so many 'County' runs that I experienced. Overall it was not bad, although it did not match either 4093 or 4087 on runs I had starting at Pontypool Road.

1011 *County of Chester* starts away from Newport High Street with the 11am Brighton-Cardiff, 18 February 1961. (J. Hodge)

Bristol Temple Meads-Shrewsbury, 5.4.1963
2.0pm Plymouth-Manchester
1021 County of Montgomery **82B**
8 vehicles, 257/280 tons Bristol-Pontypool Road
9 vehicles, 288/320 tons Pontypool Road-Shrewsbury (train full & standing)

Distance Miles	Location	Times mins secs	Speed mph	Schedule
	Bristol Temple Meads	00.00		T
	Dr Days Bridge Jcn	02.47		
	Lawrence Hill	04.00//05.15	sig stand	
	Stapleton Road	07.58		
0.0		00.00		
	Ashley Hill	03/05	23	
	Horfield	06.33	24	
	Filton Jcn	09.29	15*	
4.4	Patchway	11.35	40	
8.0	Pilning	15.51	64	
9.2	Severn Tunnel East	17.28	66/68	
	Severn Tunnel West	22.31	34	
14.9	Severn Tunnel Jcn	25.35		
0.0		00.00		
	Magor	04.30	53	
	Bishton	-	65	
	Maindee East Jcn	13.28	sigs 10*	
11.5	Caerleon	17.20	42	
	Ponthir	19.28	51	1 in 120R
	Llantarnam	21.26	40	1 in 106R
16.1	L.Pontnewydd	24.31	36/28	1 in 95R
	Panteg Jcn	-	26	
18.8	Pontypool Road	31.20		3 E
0.0		00.00		3½ L
	Little Mill	03.01	pws 40*/54	
4.1	Nantyderry	06.10	46/55	
6.7	Penpergwm	08.55	65/58*	1 in 80F
	Abergavenny	12.31	48	1 in 82R
10.4	Abergavenny Jcn	14.16	40/31	
13.4	Llanvihangel	20.35	30/33	1 in 95R
15.8	Pandy	23.31	60	1 in 100F
20.9	Pontrilas	29.45	57*/62	
	St Devereux	33.05	61	
26.7	Tram Inn	35.32	67	
30.0	Red Hill Jcn	39.17	44*	
	Rotherwas Jcn	41.35	60	
33.4	Hereford	44.05		5½ L
0.0		00.00		4 L
	Barrs Court Jcn	02.44		
	Shelwick Jcn	04.27	48/56	
4.2	Moreton-on-Lugg	07.23	61	

	Dinmore	11.03	52	1 in 100R
	Ford Bridge	14.23	62/64	
12.6	Leominster	16.45	65	
	Berringtom & Eye	20.15	59/50	
18.9	Woofferton	23.50	58	
23.5	Ludlow	30.02	42/39	
	Bromfield	32.55	51	
28.1	Onibury	35.55	56/47	1 in 112R
31.1	Craven Arms	39.38	52/35	1 in 105/130R
	Marshbrook	46.43	42	1 in 112R
38.2	Church Stretton	50.58	35/54	
41.7	Leebotwood	-	66	1 in 100F
44.6	Dorrington	-	74	1 in 90F
46.8	Condover	59.48	58*	
	Sutton Bridge Jcn	64.16		
51.0	Shrewsbury	66.59		7 L

1021 County of Montgomery at Bath with a Portsmouth-Salisbury-Bristol train, c1961. (GW Trust)

The schedule was relatively easy as far as Pontypool Road and although speed dropped rapidly on the climb to Panteg Junction, time was well in hand. However, the schedule onwards was tougher and I have the feeling that if 1021 had been free steaming, time could have been kept. The run showed every sign of the engine being eased to allow the boiler to recover, especially between Leominster and Craven Arms, husbanding effort for the climb to Church Stretton which was quite respectable, though I have had faster with twelve-coach 'Castle' hauled trains. Similarly, the 67 minute run against a schedule of 64 minutes should have been bettered.– I have had a couple of 'Castle' runs with heavy loads completed under the hour and a 'Hall' with 200 tons in 51 minutes.

1021 returned on the overnight 12.45am Manchester-Penzance, which both it and I took back to Bristol. We were both weary, for 1021 struggled on the gradients and lost time heavily arriving in Bristol 35 minutes late, presumably caused by shortage of steam.

I had a number of runs between Pontypool Road and Hereford on either the 2pm or 4pm Plymouth in April and May with 4087, 4093, 5014, 5050 and 7022, and one further run with a 'County', 1024 County of Pembroke on the eight-coach 4pm Plymouth. It was a weak effort, although there were no obvious signs that the engine was in trouble. 1024 lost two and a half minutes on the easier 46 minute schedule (the 2pm was only allowed 42 minutes) without seeming to be opened out onto the main valve of the regulator. It was taken very easily up to Llanvihangel falling to 24mph and drifted downhill the other side mainly in the mid-fifties with just a momentary 62 before the Pontrilas slowing.

I had one final effort at going through to Shrewsbury before the summer timetable and reappearance of the Brush diesels, this time on the 4.40pm Cardiff-Liverpool with Cardiff East Dock's 5092. We had an excellent run, though I regretted not returning to Hereford to pick up the 4pm Plymouth which rolled into Shrewsbury early behind 4087. I went back overnight via Bristol again expecting a 'Castle' off the 2pm Plymouth (the return working) but got a St Philips Marsh 'Hall', 4993, which, because of the heavy twelve coach load, received a Shrewsbury 'County' as pilot as far as the Church Stretton summit. 1014 *County of Glamorgan* was my last run behind a 'County' and I would like to say it was an inspiring one, but both engines plodded in the upper twenties up the long 1 in 100. Frankly, 4993 needed 1014's assistance for the rest of the night, for our arrival in Bristol was very late, similar to my previous experience with 1021.

How do I sum up my personal experience with 'Counties' and align them with that of other train recorders, especially experts like Cecil J. Allen and O.S. Nock? My experience of them was very patchy. I had as many bad runs as good – or vice versa to put it more positively. They had flashes of power over relatively short distances but were not so happy on routes that required long sustained steaming. It is a mistake to attempt to compare them with 'Castles' that some operating authorities initially seemed to by using them indiscriminately with the latter. They were most suited to the heavily graded routes west of Newton Abbot, the Bristol-Shrewsbury 'North & West' and the

1024 *County* of Pembroke at Bristol Bath Road in good condition on 28 February 1959, as it was externally in May 1963 when it was allocated to St Philips Marsh. (J. Hodge)

Wolverhampton-Chester section. If they had all been allocated there from the start and developed as specialist engines for those routes alone, with their regular link drivers, their reputation may have been better. As it was, many drivers considered the 'Modified Halls' to be Hawksworth's most successful design. Despite having smaller diameter driving wheels – 6ft instead of 6ft 3in – they seemed speedier and are credited with many runs when they reached and maintained speeds in the upper 80s. I had experience of two such runs, one of which I was on the footplate. Certainly, Old Oak men with whom I rode frequently during my BR training used to call their

'Modified Halls' *Old Oak Castles* as they so frequently were put quite satisfactorily on 81A 'Castle' diagrams on Summer Saturdays when the depot had more 'Castle' diagrams than they had 'Castles' allocated. It is of some significance that the need for more Western Region express passenger and mixed traffic power in 1948-50 resulted in further builds of the 1923 'Castle' design and the 'Modified Hall', rather than increasing the number of the 1946 'Counties'.

I will finish with quotations from Andrew Roden, editor of the monthly magazine *Steam World*, from an editorial comment on the 'strange enigma of the 6MTs'.

'As a general rule, Britain's railway companies were highly adept at designing locomotives to suit a full range of duties, but, with one and perhaps two exceptions, bridging the gap between the versatile 5MT 4-6-0s and '7P' and higher express locomotives seems to have been rather a challenge.'

After commenting about the disappointing early days of the LMS 'Jubilees' and the BR Standard 'Clan' pacifics, he goes on to write about the 'Counties':

'And what of the GWR 'County' 4-6-0s? Designed to fill the gap between the 'Halls' and the 'Castles', they were a disappointment too. With slightly larger driving wheels and slightly more power than the smaller design, on the face of it they seemed an ideal and economic solution to providing more 'oomph' on passenger duties. Yet again though, the draughting wasn't quite right, and although they were better when fitted with double

chimneys from 1955, they were in every sense, a poor man's 'Castle' from the moment they were built.'

He goes on to say :

'Draughting problems are a common factor in all three designs, but so too is tractive effort. A "Jubilee's" nominal 26,610lbs was barely an improvement on the 25,445lbs of a "Black Five". The 27,275lbs of a "Hall" wasn't much less than the 29,090lbs (after a reduction in boiler pressure) of a "County", and the 27,250lbs of the "Clans" was little better than the 26,120lbs of a "5MT"… but there was often a fair gulf between these types and the 7P designs. Could it be that the difference in classification prompted operating authorities to put heavier loads or tighter schedules on these class 6 locomotives than they were actually capable of managing?'

Andrew Roden goes on to quote the LNER V2 as the one major

exception to these comments and finishes by saying:

'The "Jubilees" were certainly numerous with almost 200 built and eventually did good work on the London Midland Region. When redraughted, the "Counties" also redeemed themselves somewhat, particularly on hilly routes with relatively low speeds. But to me they and the "Clans" remain somewhat enigmatic machines. They were different, relatively rare, and flawed. Perhaps that's why they seem to have such character to me: if to be flawed is to be human, then surely their flaws made those steam locomotives, already so alive, just that little bit more so.'

I have a couple of models of 'County' 4-6-0s, a 'Cotswold' kit that was constructed and painted in 1983 depicting the last survivor, 1011 *County of Chester*, and a 'Dapol' production as 1027 *County of Stafford* which I detailed and repainted as 1003 *County of Wilts*.

The 1983 constructed 'Cotswold' kit model of 1011 *County of Chester*. (David Maidment)

Preservation – 1014 *County of Glamorgan*

The last 'County', 1011 *County of Chester,* was withdrawn in November 1964 and the class became extinct. It was sold to Cashmore's at Newport and was scrapped in March 1965. Unfortunately, no 'Counties' were bought by Woodham's and therefore there were no locomotives of the class stored at Barry that could have been purchased for preservation.

However, the 'Counties' contained many GW standard parts and there were many GW engines stored at Barry that could provide appropriate elements. The project benefits particularly from two locomotives rescued from Woodham's by the Wales Railway Centre (the 'Barry Ten') and acquired in 2004 when that project closed. 7927 *Willington Hall*

The **1985** 'Dapol' model of 1027 converted by the author as 1003 *County of Wilts.* (David Maidment)

1014 *County of Glamorgan* in its original single chimney form, in BR mixed traffic livery – although scarcely discernible under the grime, c1955. (J.M. Bentley Collection/Real Photographs)

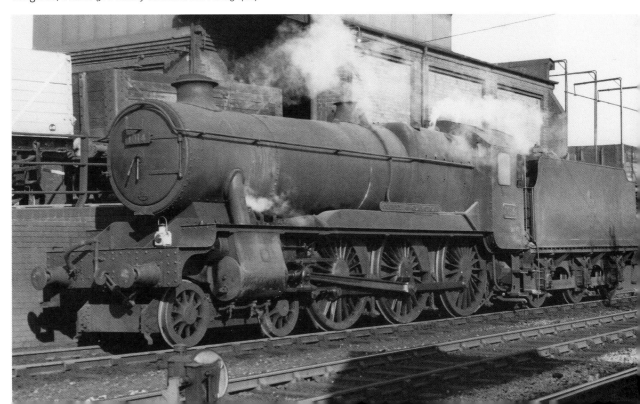

withdrawn in December 1965 has provided the frames and LMS 8F 48518, built at Doncaster in 1944, has provided the boiler which is under repair and modification at Crewe to fit the 'County' chassis in 2016.

The project is planned in four stages, the first being the modification of the Hall's frames, bogie and brake equipment and the manufacture of three sets of 6ft 3in driving wheels to create a rolling chassis. The second stage is to rebuild the 8F boiler as a standard Swindon three-row superheated No.15 boiler with smokebox and double chimney now underway in 2016. The third stage is to acquire and refurbish the motion, fittings and pipework and the final stage will be the construction of a new flush-sided Hawksworth tender.

The project is being carried out at the Didcot GW Society premises under the overall control of the GWS Chairman, Richard Croucher, and – in 2016 – needs an estimated £300,000 to complete.

1014 at Bristol Bath Road, 3 March 1957. (J.M. Bentley Collection/ R.A. Panting)

1014 *County* of *Glamorgan* at Swindon after overhaul, and repaint in the BR passenger green livery, 13 May 1961.
(R.C. Riley)

1014 shortly before withdrawal at Swindon shed. It was withdrawn in April 1964.
(GW Trust)

The new frames and wheel set at Didcot GW Centre after assembly and display on August Bank Holiday Saturday, 27 August 2016, alongside preserved 6023 *King Edward II*. (GW Society)

1014 fitted with a makeshift wooden cabside numberplate, 22 March 1964. (GW Trust/D. Cape)

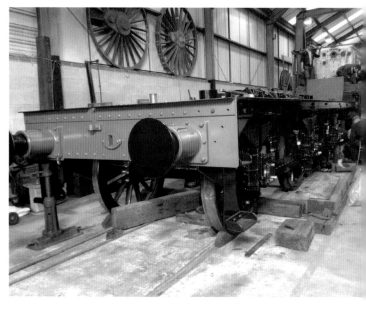

The new Hawksworth flush-sided tender under construction for 1014 at Didcot GW Centre, October 2016. (GW Society)

POSTSCRIPT

At a meeting of railway engineers who lunch together regularly at the Institute of Civil Engineers, a couple made mention of various tests carried out at Swindon in the late 1930s, particularly the possible impact of the application of Chapelon's rebuilding of the French P.O. pacific and 4-8-0. This will be particularly relevant to the book I am currently writing for Pen & Sword on the Great Western Kings, but one of my colleagues, Doug Landau, gave me a copy of a report by F.C.Mattingly, Chief Draughtsman to Frederick Hawksworth at Swindon, undated but c1946, referring to tests with double chimney 'County' No. 1000 in November and December 1945. Although the text of the book on the GW Counties has been completed, I believe this information is of sufficient interest to add an extract of Mr Mattingly's report, entitled 'Draught Arrangement on Engine No.1000.'

'As suggested in report dated 22ⁿᵈ November 1945, trials of Engine No.1000 with existing blast-pipe tips have been completed; as far as the main object of the trial is concerned, i.e. reduction of ash accumulation in the smoke-box and spark ejection from the chimney, no recommendations can be made until the larger blast-pipe tips have been tried out, although the indications are that the smoke-box vacuum cannot be much reduced without loss of performance. Some useful information has however already been gained from the trials so far completed:-

1. The Hopper-type Ash-pan is causing undue restriction to the air-flow through the grate; available I.H.P. was increased by over 500 by clamping the hopper door open to the extent of about 1".
2. With hopper doors clamped in this position, maximum I.H.P. recorded was about 2,000, which is 33% more than was expected from calculations made on the assumption that performance would be similar to that of other 2-cyl GWR locomotives of roughly comparable dimensions.
3. Maximum I.H.P. was obtained at speeds of at least 300 R.P.M. (ie 67 mph) instead of about 240 R.P.M. as has been found to be the case with other classes.
4. In order to enable full advantage to be taken of the considerably increased power of this engine, later cut-offs should be maintained at higher speeds than is the normal practice of drivers on 2-cyl. engines.
5. At no time during the trial with hopper-doors clamped open was there any indication that the limit of boiler capacity was approached.

Trials on December 4ᵗʰ and 11ᵗʰ were carried out with a tare load of 416 tons, and on December 12ᵗʰ with 391 tons (43 and 20 tons respectively in excess of 'Castle' load for Brimscombe Bank); coal was of poor quality on December 4ᵗʰ, but of moderately good quality on December 11ᵗʰ and 12ᵗʰ; hopper doors were closed on 4th and 11ᵗʰ, and clamped about 1" open on 12th …. Throughout the series of trials, the safety valves were blowing off at about 265 lbs psi on the gauge.

On no occasion was any difficulty experienced in the ascent of Brimscombe Bank; boiler pressure was maintained each time, but there was clearly more in hand on the 12ᵗʰ, when the top of the steepest part of the bank was reached with safety valves blowing off, firehole door open, and water level maintained; on this occasion the lowest speed on the bank was 32 mph.

At higher speeds there was some difficulty in maintaining boiler pressure with hopper-doors closed; in fact the performance under these conditions… could not be sustained with an injector on; it was observed that the fire was not burning satisfactorily in the back half of the box. With hopper-doors open, however, maximum power appeared to be capable of being maintained indefinitely….

Acceleration from 60 to 72 mph corresponded to a power of 1900 – 2000 I.H.P. on each of the three runs.

The low values of I.H.P. recorded between speeds of 30 and 50 mph appear to be due to the practice of working back to 25% cut-off at about 40 mph. The results of the trial indicate that full advantage can be taken of the power available if the following method of working is adhered to:

45%	cut-off not to be	
	used at speeds below	20 mph.
40%	- " -	30 mph
35%	- " -	40 mph
30%	- " -	50 mph
25%	- " -	60 mph

Certain inferences can already be drawn from the records of these trials…… boiler output is ultimately determined by blast-pipe efficiency…. It is estimated that the draught necessary to produce 2000 I.H.P. on '1000' class engines

is about 10" of water; the smoke-box vacuum recorded on No.1000 at this power output was 11" – 12", which does not give much margin. However it should be noted that the present blast pipe tips were designed to give a steam velocity of 1000ft ./ sec. at an output of 1410 I.H.P. At 2000 I.H.P. the velocity increases to 1450 ft./sec., and the back-pressure to 12.5 lbs/sq in.

Tips of 4 ¼ " diameter would reduce the back-pressure to 6.5 lbs psi representing a saving of 140 I.H.P at 65 mph. It may well be that this saving will compensate for the drop in vacuum consequent upon the drop in steam velocity. This size of tip gives a maximum velocity of 1150 ft./sec and would enable this orifice to be raised about 3" above its present position…..

It may further be inferred that the fitting of a double blast-pipe to other classes of engine will enable power output to be increased to at least 70 I.H.P. per sq ft of grate area at 300 RPM provided that areas

of steam passages, particularly through the superheater, are increased accordingly. The present power available on 4-cyl engines is 45-50 I.H.P. per sq ft, so the increase would be greater than has been achieved on engine 1000, as compared with the power that was expected from that engine - ie 54 I.H.P. per sq ft. – although in fact the performance of other '1000' class engines does not suggest that these expectations are likely to be realised in their present form, because the draught is not sufficient to give the necessary higher rate of combustion…..'

The report concludes that a double blast-pipe to increase power output to 70 I.H.P. per grate area sq ft. would be even more effective in increasing the power of the 'Castles' by 40% and the 'Kings' by 45%. It is disappointing in the light of this that it took nearly ten further years before that lesson was applied, not only to the Kings and Castles, but also the other Counties.

APPENDICES

County Class 4-4-0s

Dimensions

Cylinders (2):	18″ x 30″
Coupled wheels:	6′ 8½″
Bogie wheels:	3′ 2″
Valve gear:	Stephenson
Heating surface:	1,818.12 sq ft
Grate area:	20.56 sq ft
Boiler pressure:	200 lbs psi
Axle load	18 tons 3 cwt
Weight, Engine:	55 tons 6 cwt
Tender:	36 tons 15 cwt
Total:	92 tons 1 cwt
Tender capacity:	4 tons of coal, 3,000 gallons of water
Tractive effort (85%):	20,530 lbs

Weight Diagram

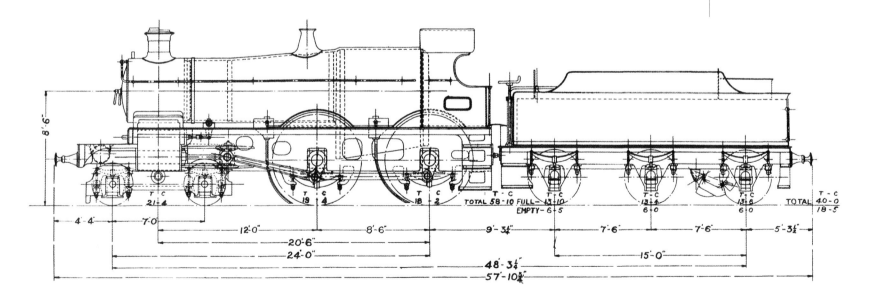

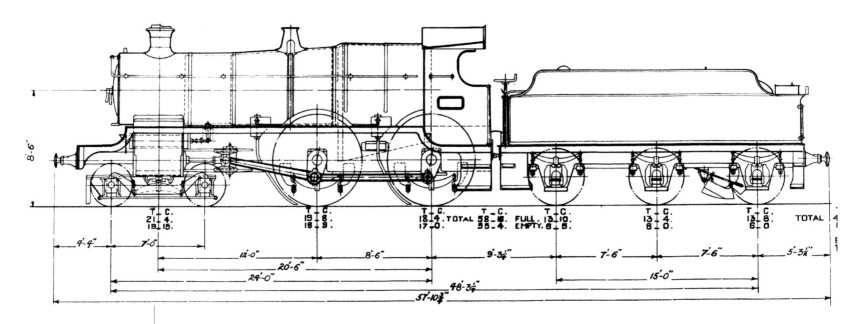

Statistics

No.	Name	Built	First depot	Last depot	Withdrawal	Mileage
3800*	*County of Middlesex*	5/04	Westbourne Park	Weston- Super- Mare	3/31	947,691
3801	*County Carlow*	10/06	Old Oak Common	Westbury	4/31	875,973
3802	*County Clare*	10/06	Old Oak Common	Bristol Bath Road	5/31	934,271
3803	*County Cork*	10/06	Old Oak Common	Oxford	1/32	972,209
3804	*County Dublin*	10/06	Old Oak Common	Oxford	3/31	915,475
3805	*County Kerry*	10/06	Cardiff Canton	Oxford	5/33	995,962
3806	*County Kildare*	11/06	Cardiff Canton	Tyseley	2/31	841,426
3807	*County Kilkenny*	11/06	Old Oak Common	Didcot	12/30	932,111
3808	*County Limerick*	11/06	Cardiff Canton	Bristol Bath Road	10/31	985,353
3809	*County Wexford*	11/06	Old Oak Common	Leamington	9/31	991,885
3810	*County Wicklow*	11/06	Old Oak Common	Swindon	3/31	971,542
3811	*County of Bucks*	11/06	Old Oak Common	Oxford	1/31	869,498
3812	*County of Cardigan*	11/06	Cardiff Canton	Hereford	7/32	1.018,221
3813	*County of Carmarthen*	11/06	Swansea Landore	Didcot	11/31	972,960
3814	*County of Chester*	11/06	Shrewsbury	Reading	6/33	973,732
3815	*County of Hants*	11/06	Bristol Bath Road	Leamington	1/32	952.227
3816	*County of Leicester*	12/06	Bristol Bath Road	Swindon	9/31	931,712
3817	*County of Monmouth*	12/06	Cardiff Canton	Swindon	1/31	840,374
3818	*County of Radnor*	12/06	Exeter	Swindon	8/31	915685
3819	*County of Salop*	12/06	Shrewsbury	Bristol Bath	5/31	910926
3820	*County of Worcester*	12/06	Stafford Road	Reading	5/31	848,251
3821	*County of Bedford*	12/11	Stafford Road	Leamington	9/31	690,385
3822	*County of Brecon*	12/11	Stafford Road	Pontypool Road	4/33	771,904
3823	*County of Carnarvon*	12/11	Swindon	Swindon	4/31	780,310
3824	*County of Cornwall*	12/11	Bristol Bath Road	Hereford	3/31	710,623
3825	*County of Denbigh*	12/11	Stafford Road	Reading	3/31	744,980

No.	Name	Built	First depot	Last depot	Withdrawal	Mileage
3826	*County of Flint*	1/12	Stafford Road	Oxford	8/31	759,158
3827	*County of Gloucester*	1/12	Bristol Bath Road	Reading	12/31	721,587
3828	*County of Hereford*	1/12	Stafford Road	Oxford	3/33	794,306
3829	*County of Merioneth*	1/12	Stafford Road	Oxford	2/32	825,707
3830	*County of Oxford*	1/12	Stafford Road	Reading	3/31	735,056
3831 (3474)	*County of Berks*	6/04	Bristol Bath Road	Tyseley	11/30	945,012
3832 (3475)	*County of Wilts*	6/04	Westbourne Park	Oxford	5/30	1,014,175
3833 (3476)	*County of Dorset*	8/04	Bristol Bath Road	Swindon	2/30	932,028
3834 (3477)	*County of Somerset*	8/04	Bristol Bath Road	Tyseley	11/33	1,003,593
3835 (3478)	*County of Devon*	8/04	Newton Abbot	Oxford	1/31	961,113
3836 (3479)	*County of Warwick*	10/04	Westbourne Park	Stafford Road	11/31	1,044,235
3837 (3480)	*County of Stafford*	10/04	Westbourne Park	Swindon	3/31	923,923
3838 (3481)	*County of Glamorgan*	10/04	Westbourne Park	Swindon	8/30	960,345
3839 (3482)	*County of Pembroke*	10/04	Westbourne Park	Weston–super–Mare	3/30	976,677

* 3800 built as 3473, 3831 - 3839 built as 3474 - 3482 respectively

2221 Class 4-4-2T (County Tanks)
Dimensions
Cylinders (2)	18″ x 30″
Coupled wheel:	6′ 8½″
Bogie wheels:	3′ 2″
Trailing wheels:	3′ 8″
Heating surface:	1,517.89sqft
Grate area:	20.35sqft
Boiler pressure:	195lbs psi
Axle-weight:	19 tons
Total weight:	75 tons
Tractive effort (85%):	20,010lbs
Tank capacity:	2,000 gallons of water
Bunker capacity:	3 tons of coal

Weight Diagram

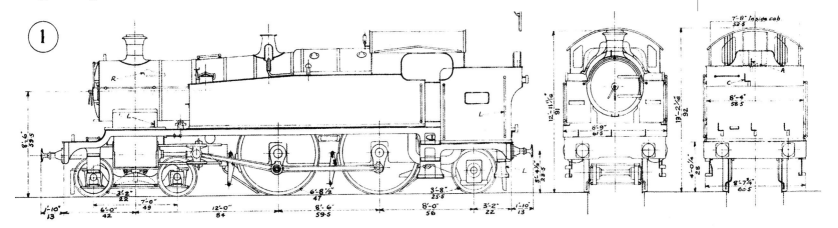

Statistics

No	Built	First Allocation	Final Allocation	Withdrawn	Final Mileage
2221	9/05	Trowbridge	Reading	9/33	641239
2222	8/06	Old Oak Common	Didcot	11/34	855,973
2223	9/06	Old Oak Common	Old Oak Common	4/32	864,770
2224	9/06	Old Oak Common	Old Oak Common	9/33	819,194
2225	9/06	Old Oak Common	Carmarthen	11/34	865,958
2226	10/06	Old Oak Common	Old Oak Common	6/34	875,317
2227	10/06	Old Oak Common	Swindon	6/31	787,517
2228	10/06	Old Oak Common	Slough	1/31	773,016
2229	10/06	Old Oak Common	Reading	1/32	795,763
2230	10/06	Basingstoke	Reading	9/32	752,009
2231	9/08	Reading	Slough	6/31	751,851
2232	9/08	Reading	Old Oak Common	10/33	841,920
2233	10/08	Reading	Reading	10/32	819,127
2234	10/08	Slough	Old Oak Common	1/32	779,383
2235	11/08	Reading	Reading	1/35	801,384
2236	11/08	Reading	Old Oak Common	1/32	739,757
2237	11/08	Old Oak Common	Old Oak Common	6/31	804,141
2238	12/08	Old Oak Common	Slough	7/31	743,578
2239	1/09	Old Oak Common	Reading	11/34	872,778
2240	1/09	Old Oak Common	Slough	11/31	763,113
2241	6/12	Basingstoke	Swindon	5/31	582,906
2242	6/12	Old Oak Common	Swindon	9/35	764,065
2243	6/12	Old Oak Common	Old Oak Common ``	11/34	783,234
2244	6/12	Old Oak Common	Reading	8/33	699,909
2245	6/12	Aylesbury	Slough	3/31	662,883
2246	6/12	Old Oak Common	Old Oak Common	11/35	782.073
2247	7/12	Old Oak Common	Reading	10/33	664,434
2248	7/12	Old Oak Common	Old Oak Common	10/31	671,435
2249	8/12	Slough	Reading	8/32	696,360
2250	8/12	Old Oak Common	Old Oak Common	2/34	726,496

4600 Churchward 4-4-2T

Dimensions

Cylinders (2)	17" x 24"
Coupled wheels:	5' 8"
Bogie wheels:	3' 2"
Trailing wheels:	3' 2"
Heating surface:	1,271.86sqft
Grate area:	16.6sqft
Boiler pressure:	200lbs psi
Axle-load:	16 tons
Total weight:	60 tons 12 cwt
Tank capacity:	1,100 gallons of water
Tractive effort (85%):	17,340lbs

Weight Diagram

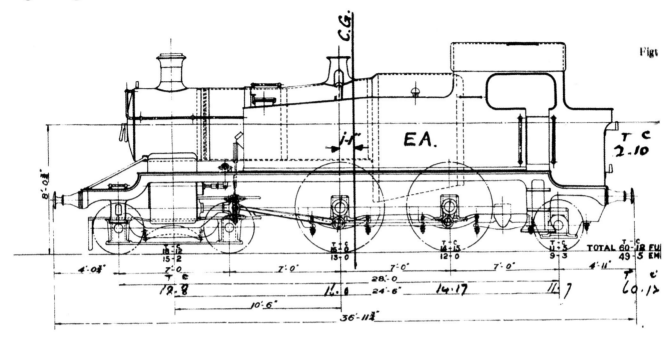

Statistics

No.	Built	First depot	Last depot	Withdrawn	Mileage
4600	11/13	Tyseley	Neyland	7/25	248,458

Proposed Churchward 4-4-4T

This proposal was for an extended version of the 'County' tank with larger bunker, but although a drawing exists, no dimension details have been found. It is assumed that most of the dimensions, apart from tank and bunker capacity and overall weight would have been similar to that of the 4-4-2Ts.

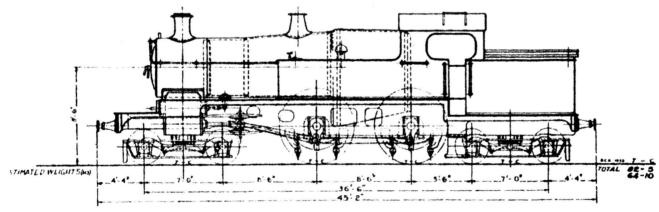

4-4-4T (circa 1905)
heavier alternative to the 2221 class

Hawksworth County Class 4-6-0

Dimensions

Cylinders (2):	18½" x 30"
Coupled wheels:	6' 3"
Bogie wheels:	3' 0"
Valve gear:	Stephenson
Heating surface:	1,979sqft
Grate area:	28.84sqft
Boiler pressure:	280lbs psi (reduced later to 250lbs psi)
Axle-load:	19 tons 14 cwt
Weight, Engine:	76 tons 17 cwt
Tender:	49 tons 0 cwt
Total:	125 tons 17 cwt
Tender capacity:	7 tons coal, 4,000 gallons water
Tractive effort (85%)	32,580lbs

Weight Diagram

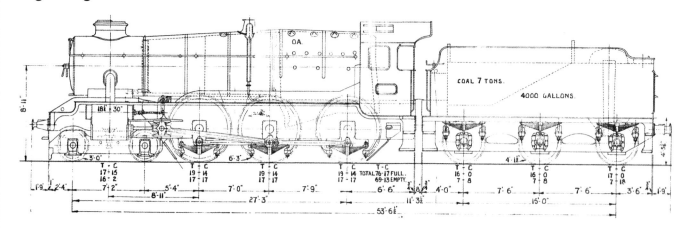

Statistics

No	Name	Date Built	D/C	First Allocation	Last Allocation	Withdrawn	Mileage
1000	County of Middlesex	8/45	3/58	Old Oak Common	Bristol SPM	7/64	733.933
1001	County of Bucks	9/45	12/57	Newton Abbot	Neyland	5/63	664,361
1002	County of Berks	9/45	6/58	Bristol Bath Road	Shrewsbury	9/63	766,263
1003	County of Wilts	10/45	11/57	Old Oak Common	Shrewsbury	10/62	655,000
1004	County of Somerset	10/45	4/57	Plymouth Laira	Swindon	10/62	657,523
1005	County of Devon	11/45	12/58	Bristol Bath Road	Bristol SPM	6/63	710,034
1006	County of Cornwall	11/45	12/58	Plymouth Laira	Swindon	9/63	687,685
1007	County of Brecknock	12/45	5/57	Bristol Bath Road	Didcot	10/62	658,967
1008	County of Cardigan	12/45	5/58	Old Oak Common	Shrewsbury	10/63	726,835
1009	County of Carmarthen	12/45	7/54*	Plymouth Laira	Bristol SPM	2/63	702,148
1010	County of Caernarvon	1/46	1/57	Old Oak Common	Swindon	7/64	779.055
1011	County of Chester	1/46	11/58	Bristol Bath Road	Bristol SPM	11/64	728,610
1012	County of Denbigh	2/46	9/57	Old Oak Common	Swindon	4/64	794,555
1013	County of Dorset	2/46	2/58	Bristol Bath Road	Swindon	7/64	630,737

No	Name	Date Built	D/C	First Allocation	Last Allocation	Withdrawn	Mileage
1014	*County of Glamorgan*	2/46	1957	Bristol Bath Road	Shrewsbury	4/64	756,762
1015	*County of Gloucester*	3/46	11/58	Old Oak Common	Plymouth Laira	11/62	724,192
1016	*County of Hants*	3/46	3/57	Stafford Road	Shrewsbury	9/63	642,078
1017	*County of Hereford*	3/46	3/59	Stafford Road	Shrewsbury	12/62	601,066
1018	*County of Leicester*	3/46	1/59	Newton Abbot	Didcot	9/62	680,979
1019	*County of Merioneth*	4/46	3/59	Newton Abbot	Shrewsbury	2/63	662,550
1020	*County of Monmouth*	12/46	11/58	Chester	Swindon	2/64	599,291
1021	*County of Montgomery*	12/46	10/59	Old Oak Common	Bristol SPM	11/63	747,716
1022	*County of Northampton*	12/46	5/56	Penzance	Shrewsbury	10/62	590,659
1023	*County of Oxford*	12/46	5/57	Truro	Shrewsbury	3/63	592,957
1024	*County of Pembroke*	1/47	7/58	Stafford Road	Swindon	4/64	643,975
1025	*County of Radnor*	1/47	8/59	Stafford Road	Shrewsbury	2/63	610,069
1026	*County of Salop*	1/47	10/58	Old Oak Common	Shrewsbury	9/62	621,007
1027	*County of Stafford*	3/47	9/56	Westbury	Swindon	10/63	650,666
1028	*County of Warwick*	3/47	8/58	Old Oak Common	Swindon	12/63	723,639
1029	*County of Worcester*	4/47	5/59	Stafford Road	Swindon	12/62	555,216

* 1009 was fitted experimentally with a stovepipe double-chimney in 7/54, undertook road tests and in 9/56 was fitted with the standard double-chimney design that evolved for the 10XX.

BIBLIOGRAPHY

COOK, K.L., *Swindon Steam 1921-1951*, 1974, Ian Allan

HARESNAPE, Brian & **SWAIN**, Alec, *Churchward Locomotives*, 1975 Ian Allan

HARESNAPE, Brian & **SWAIN**, Alec, *Collett and Hawksworth Locomotives*, , 1978, Ian Allan

NOCK O.S., *4000 Miles on the Footplate*, 1952, Ian Allan

NOCK, O.S., *Fifty Years of Western Express Running*, 1954, Edward Everard

NOCK, O.S, *Standard Gauge Great Western 4-4-0s Part 2 : 'Counties' to the close, 1904 -1961*, David & Charles 1978

RCTS, *Locomotives of the Great Western Railway, Parts 1 – 7 & 12*, 1951, RCTS

ROWLEDGE, J.W.P., *GWR Locomotive Allocations, First & Last Sheds, 1922 – 1967*, David & Charles 1986

RUSSELL, J.H., *Great Western Engines, A Pictorial Record*, Oxford Publishing Company 1978

SIXSMITH, Ian, *The Book of the County 4-6-0s*, 2012 Irwell Press

INDEX